Sacred Heart

Coloring Book

COAST COLORING BOOKS

Copyright

Copyright © 2020 by Coast Coloring Books.

All rights reserved.

Sacred Heart Coloring Book is a new first work, first published by Coast Coloring Books in 2020.

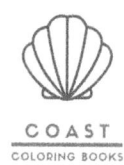

COAST
COLORING BOOKS

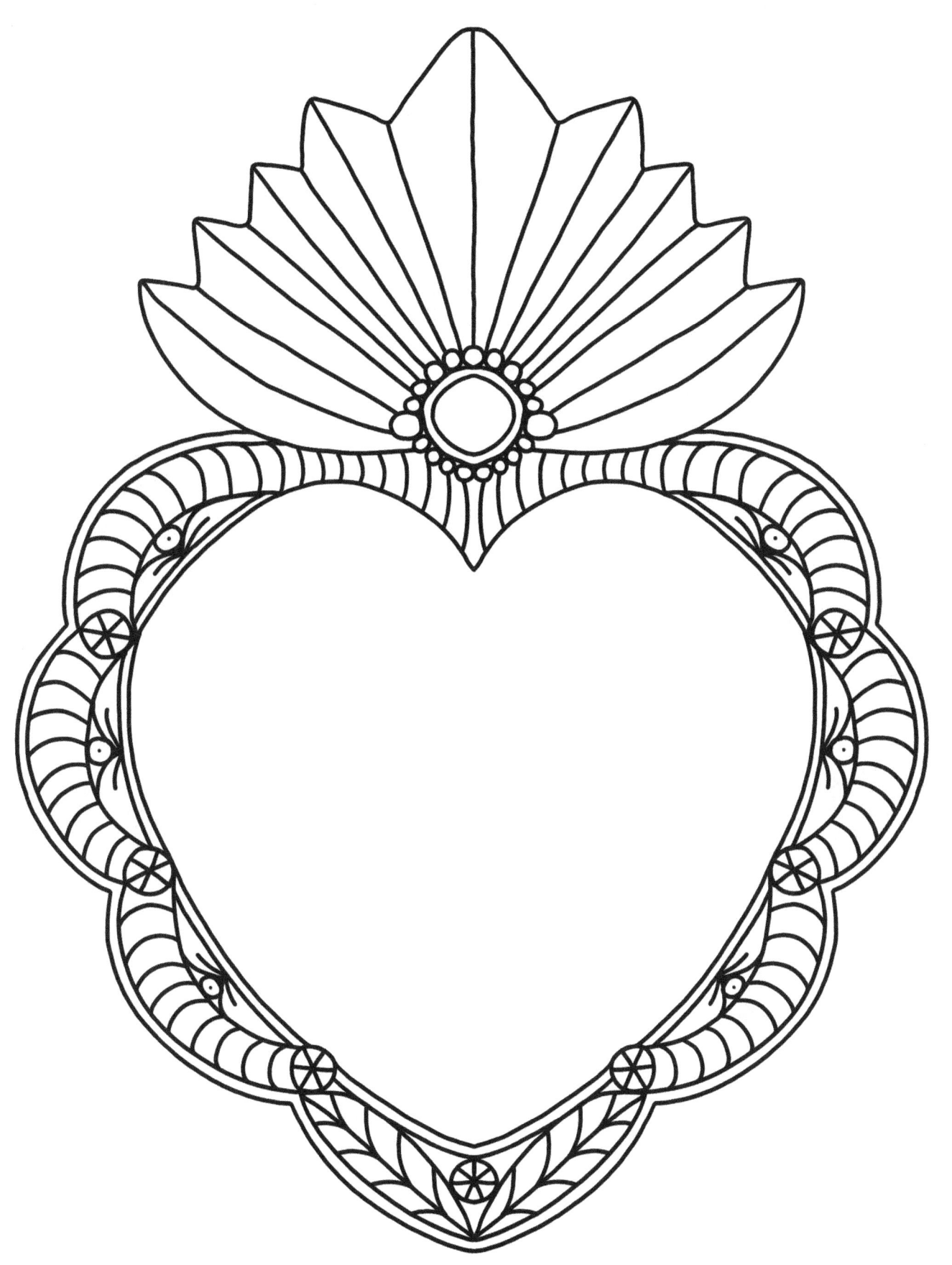

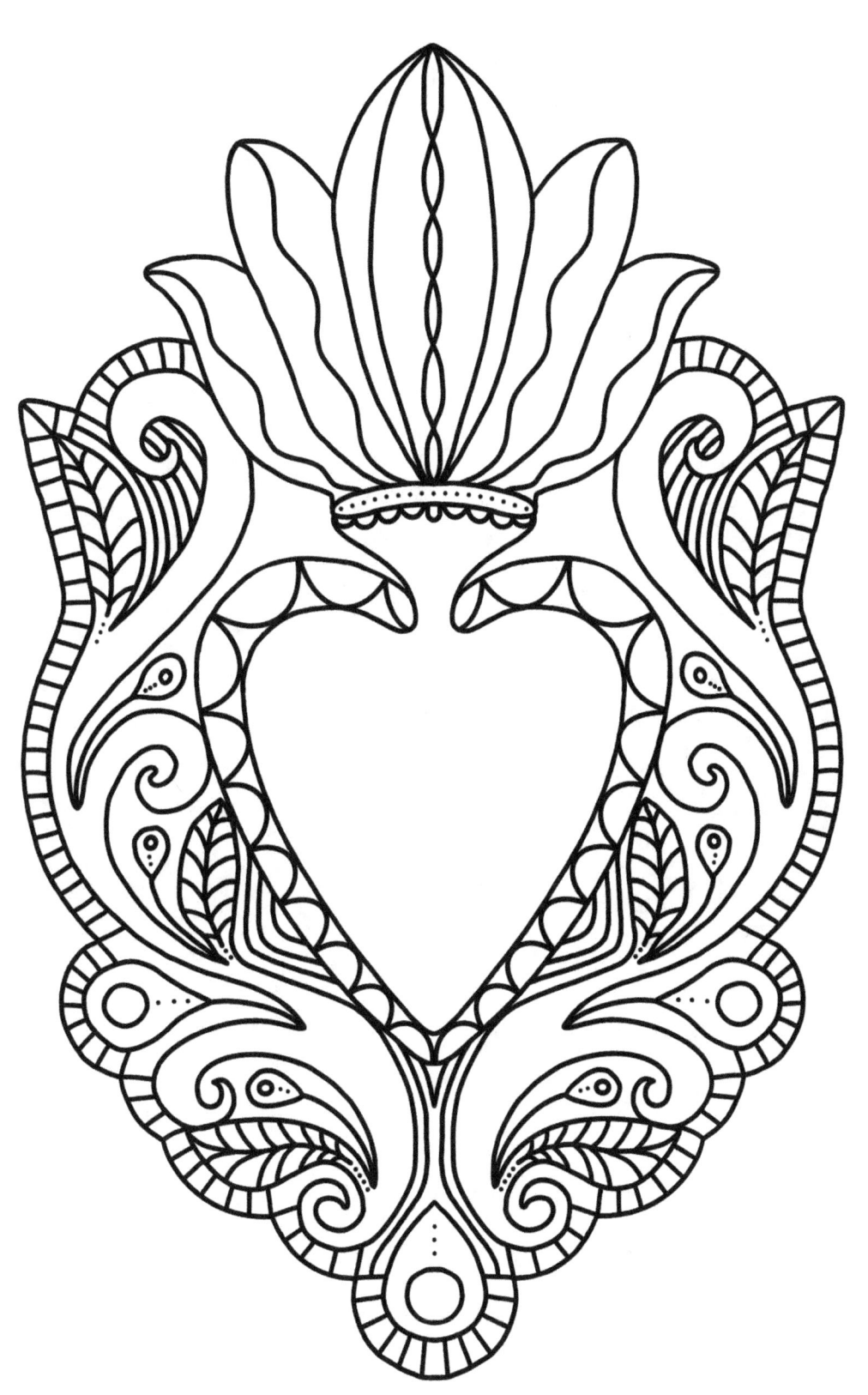

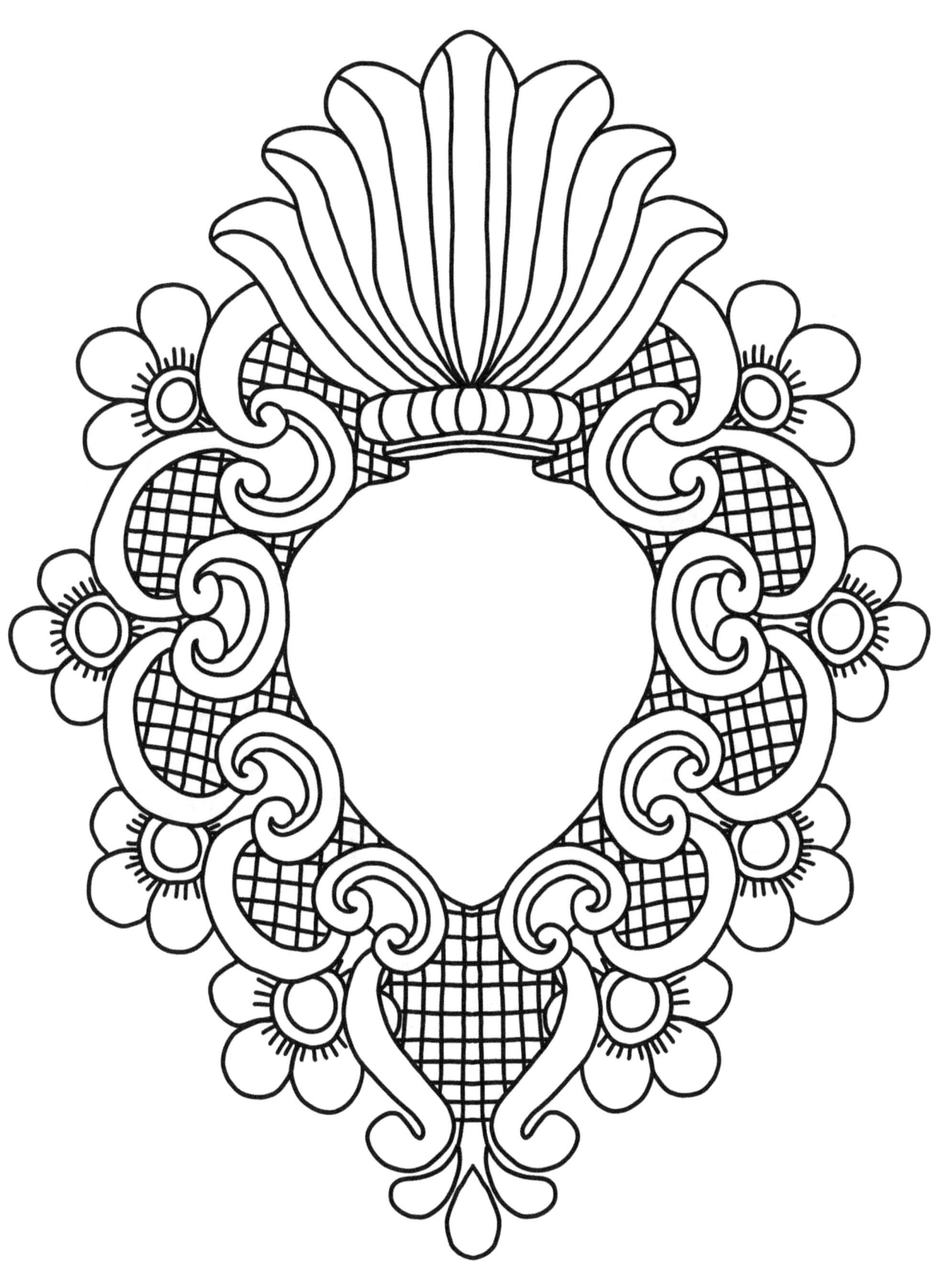

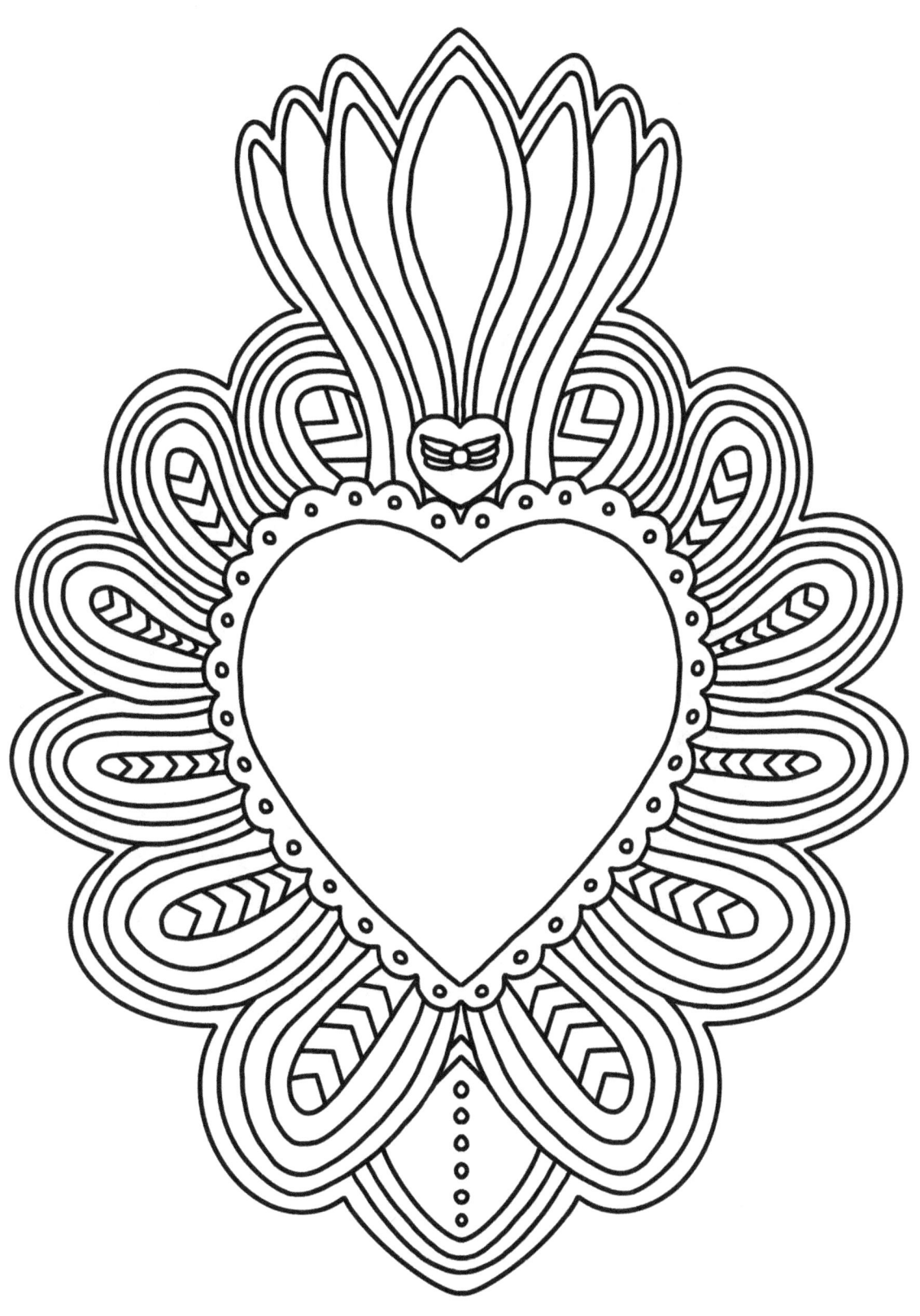

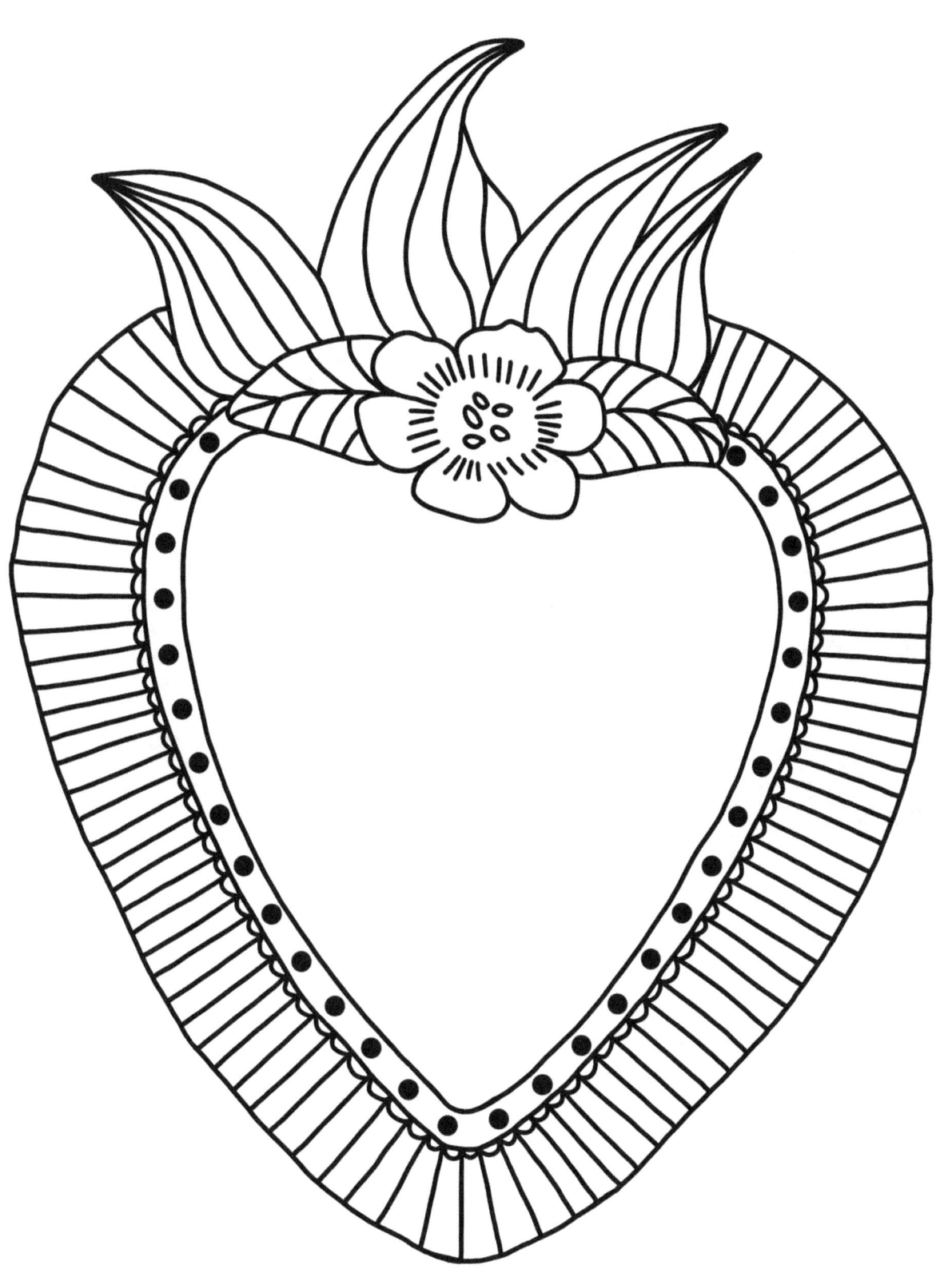

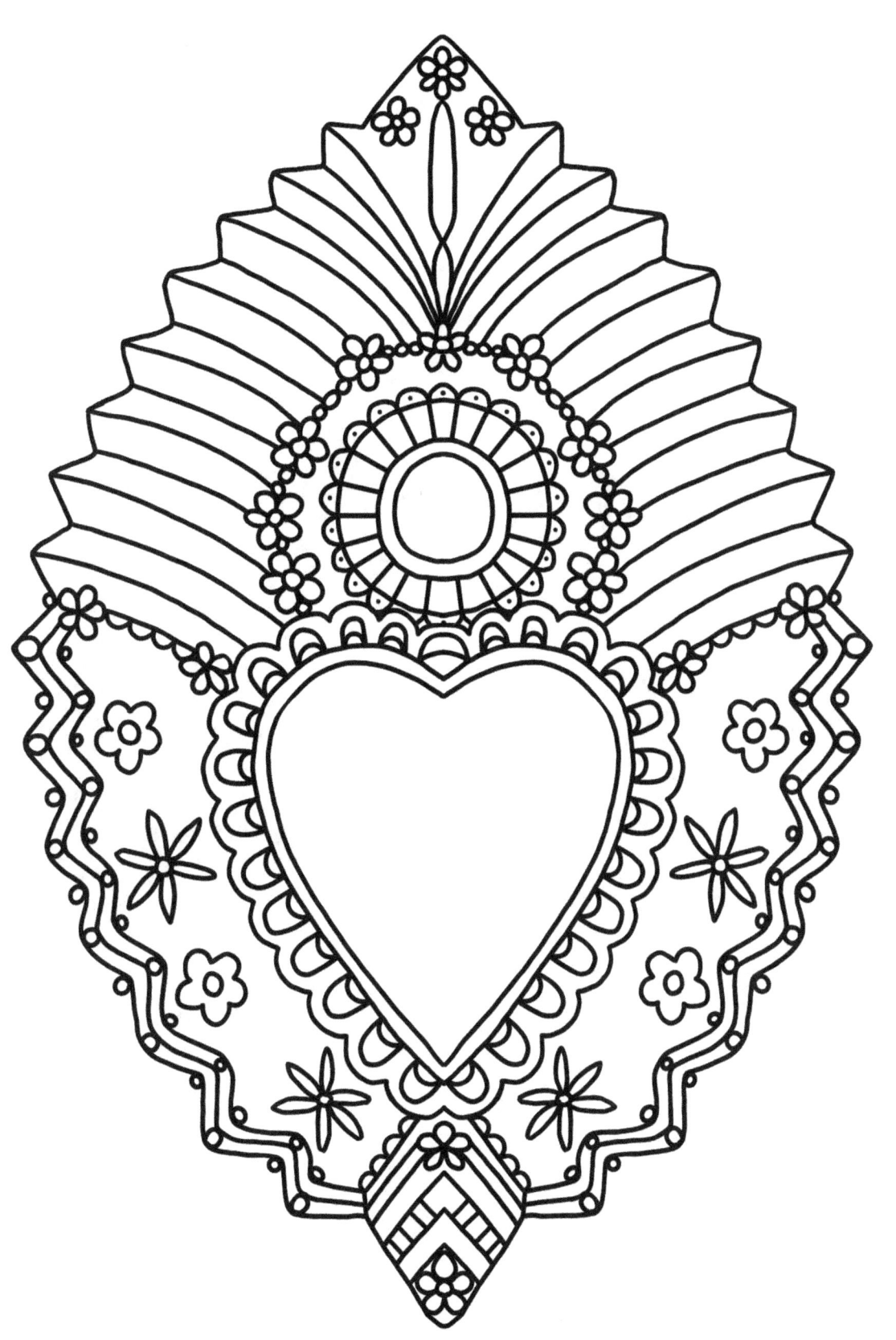

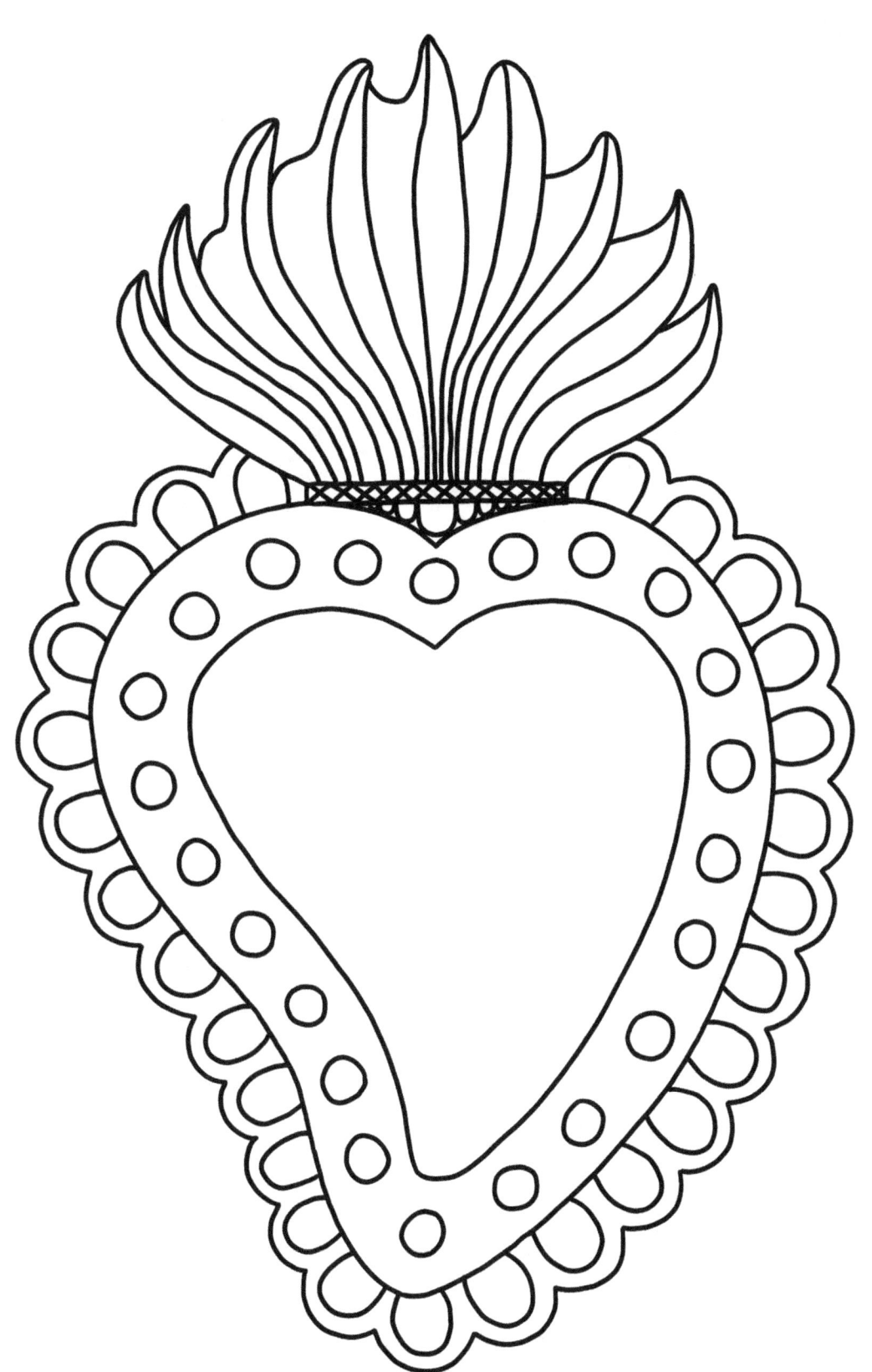

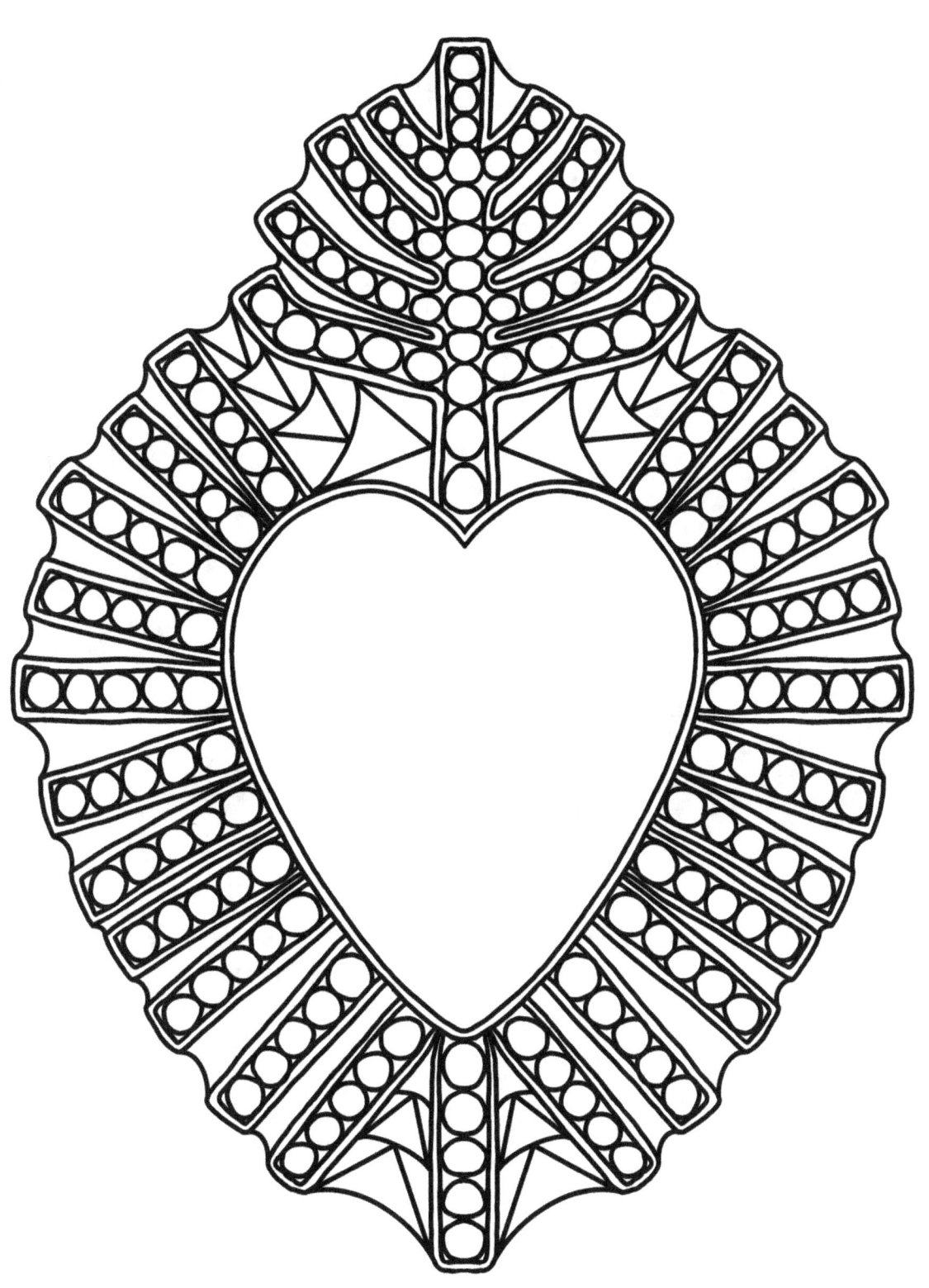

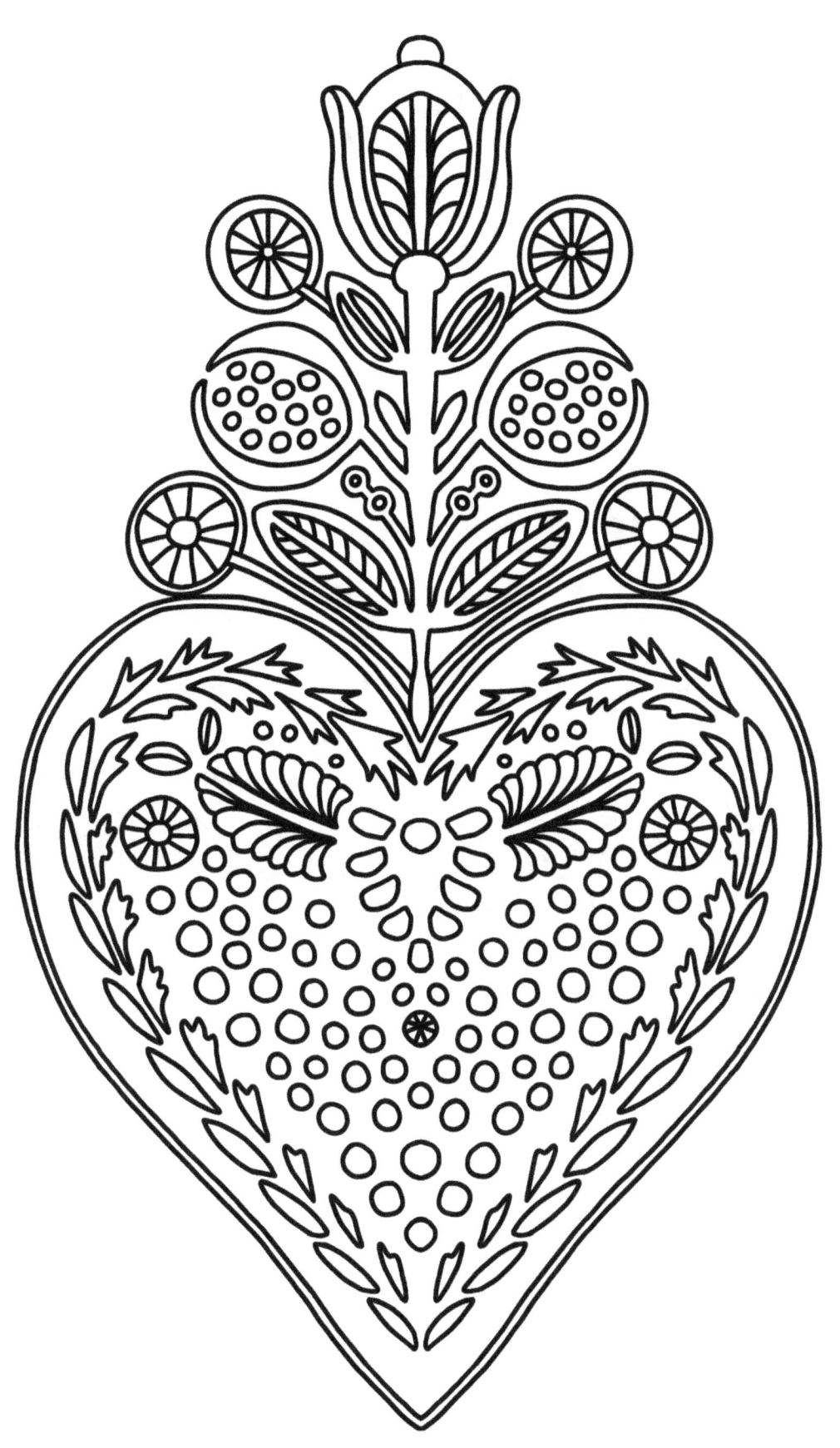

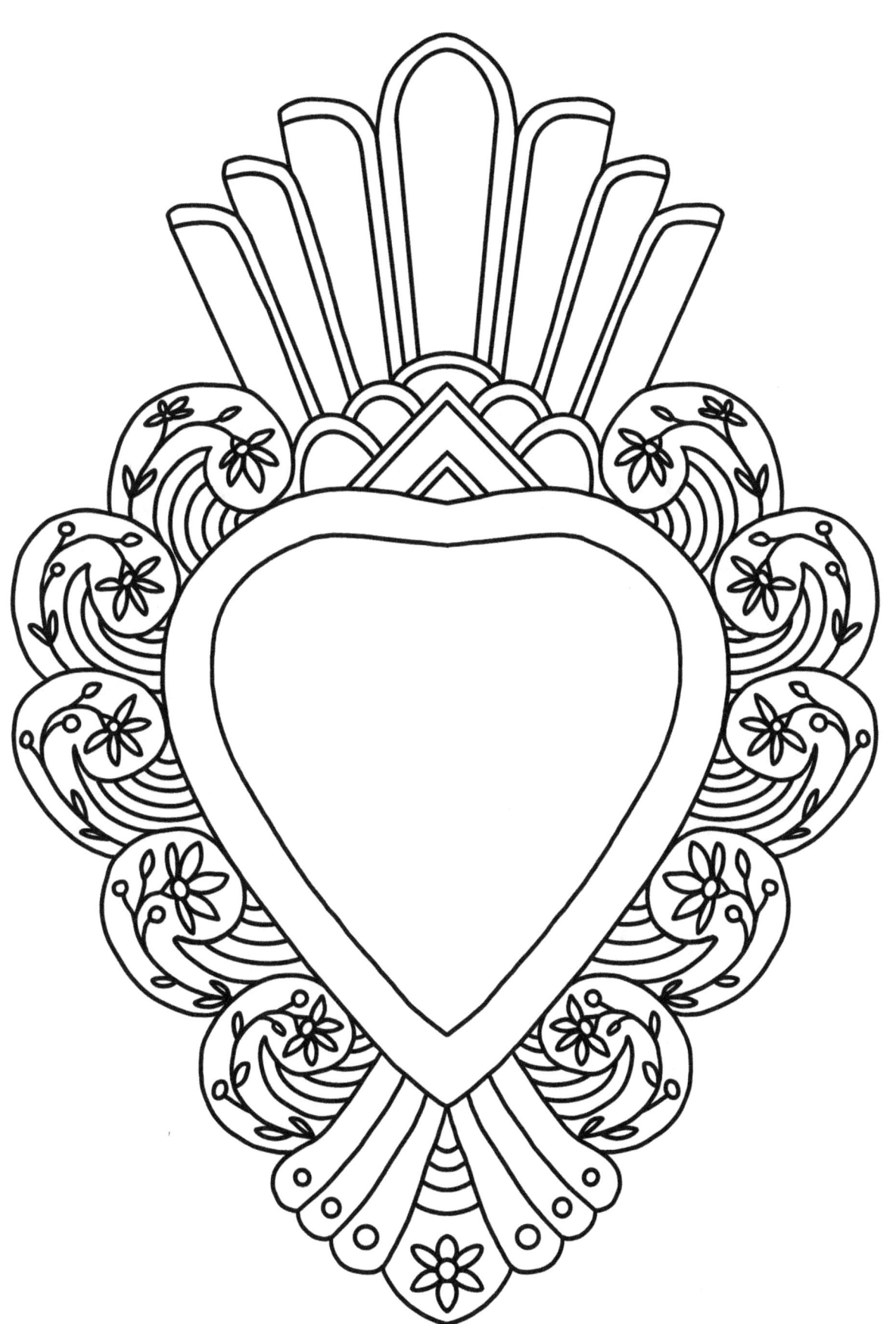

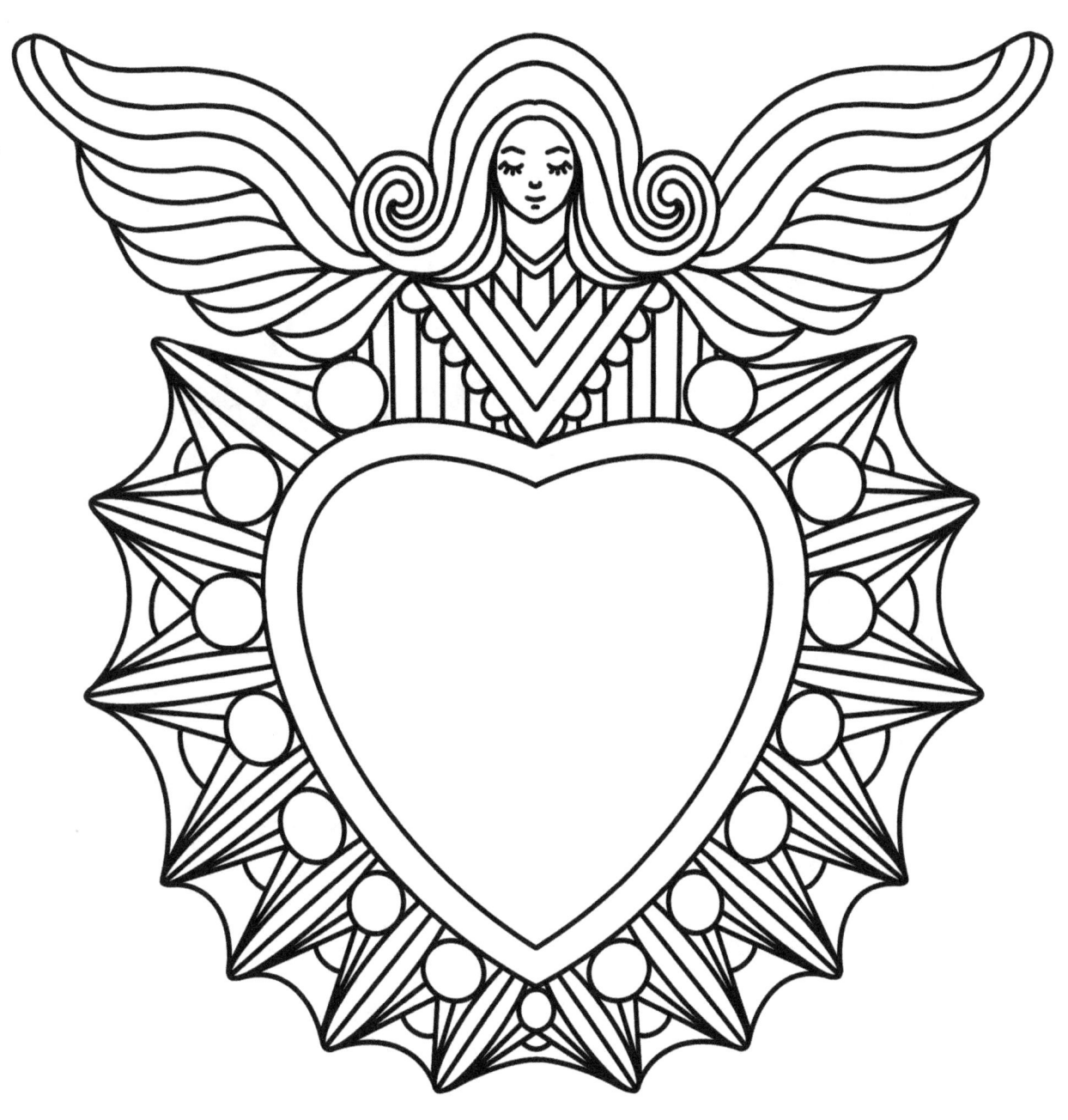

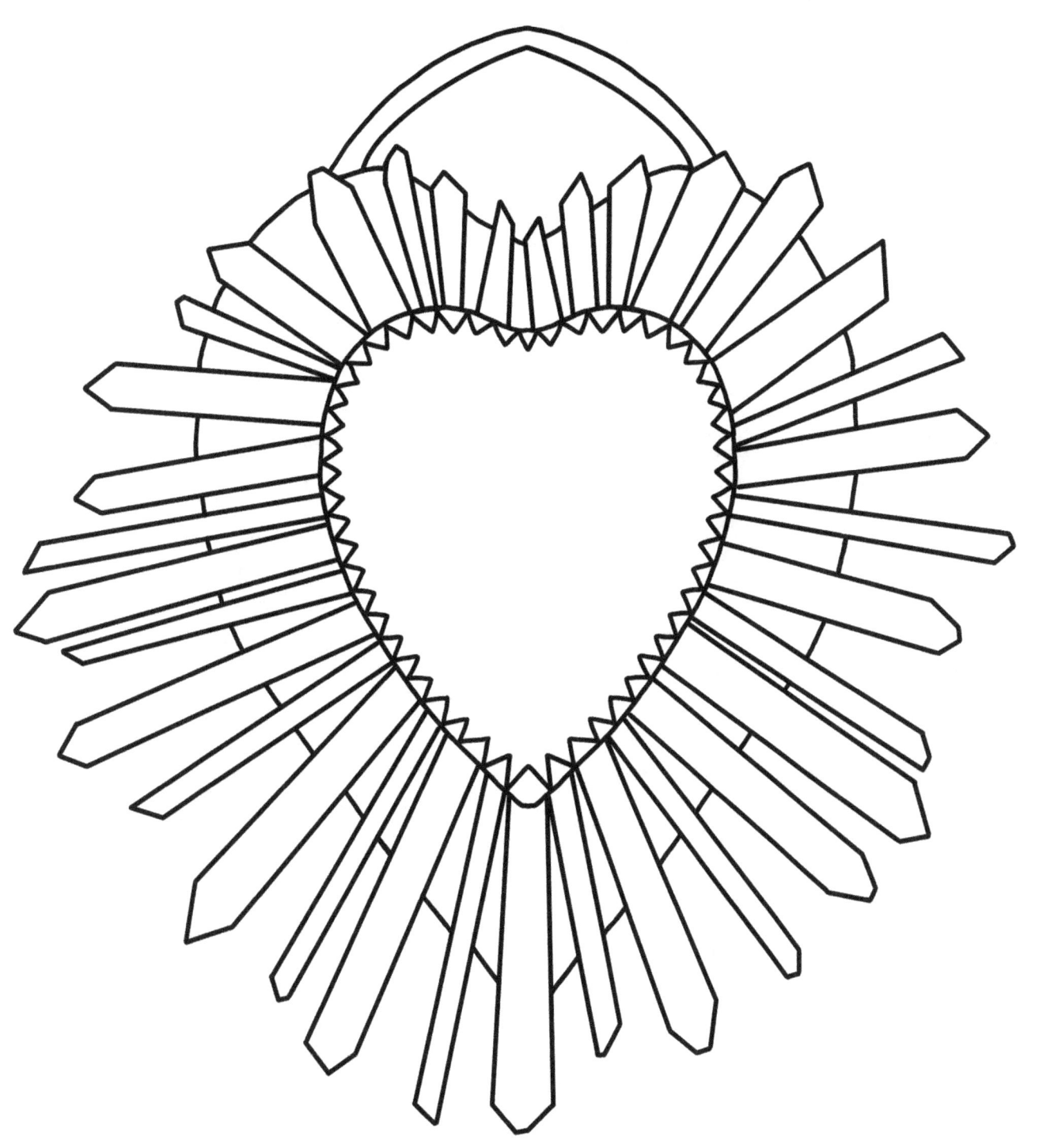

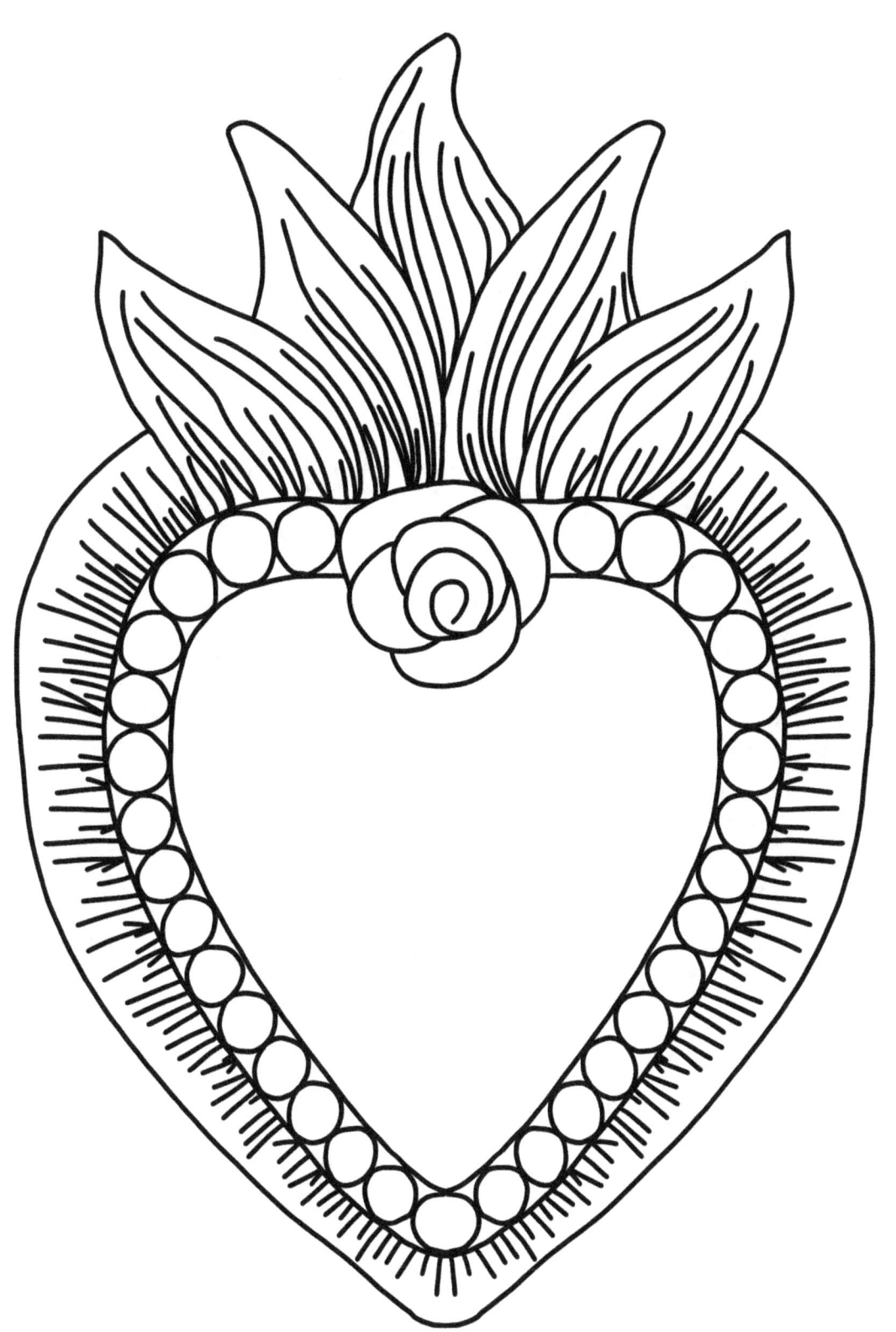

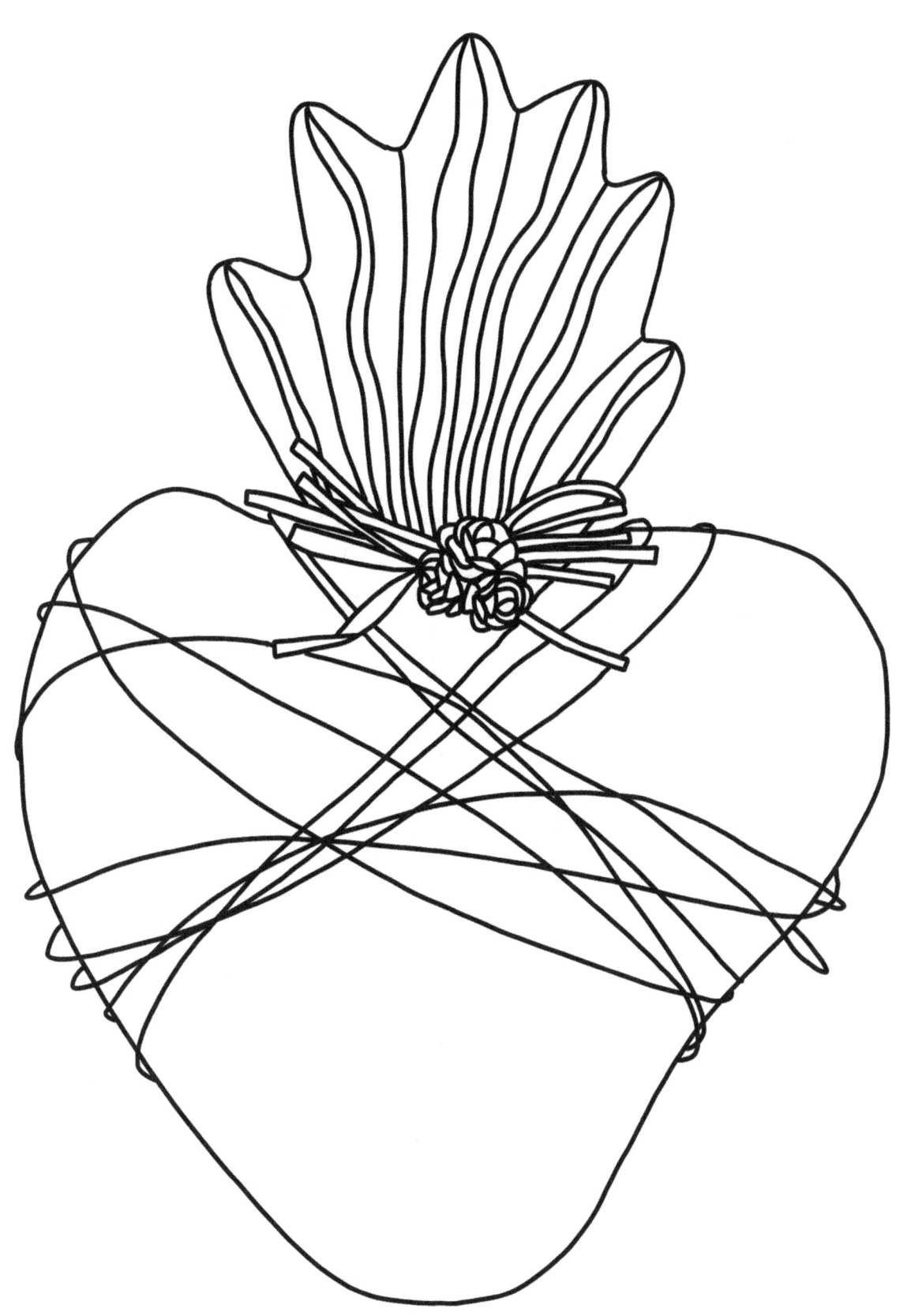

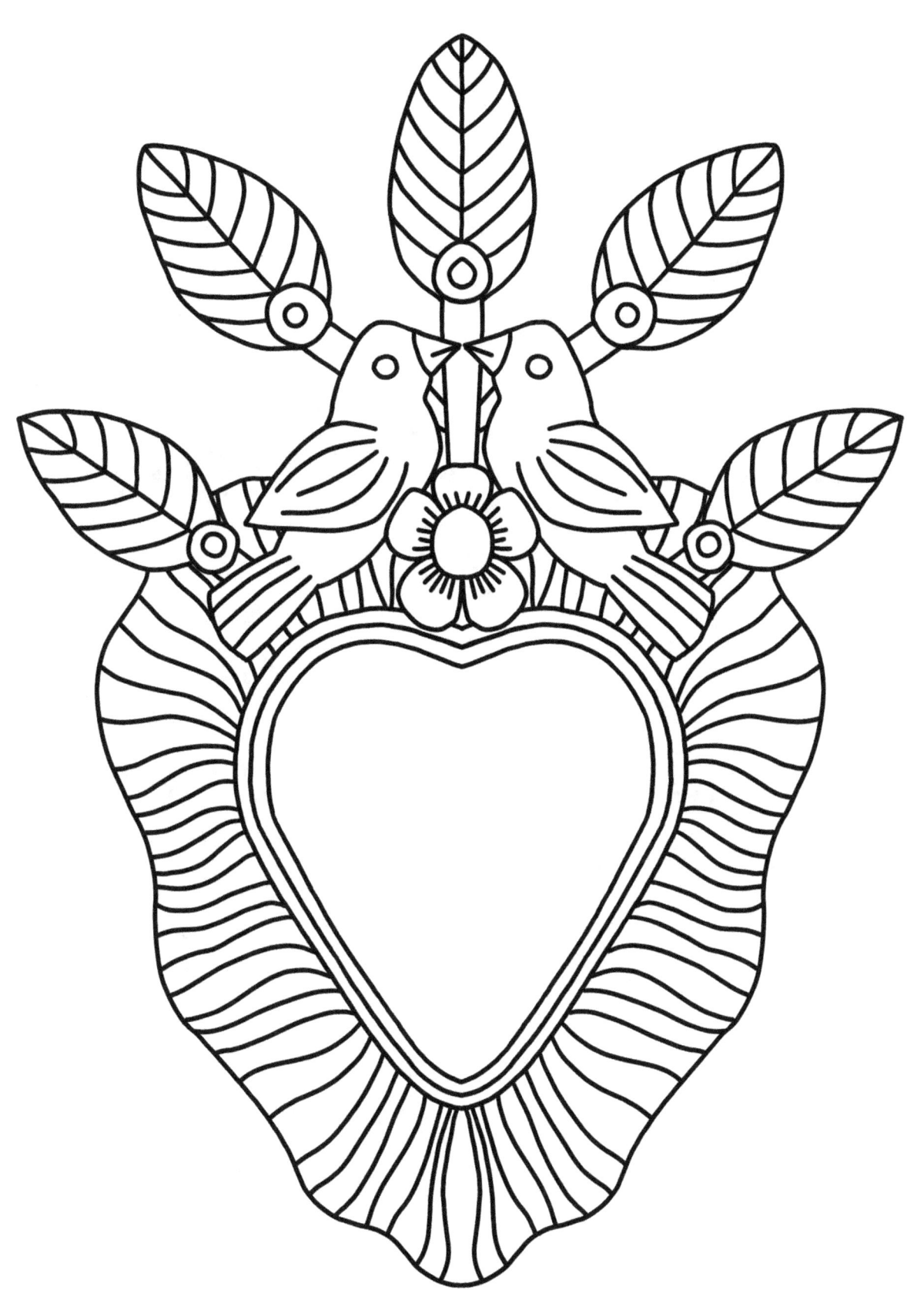

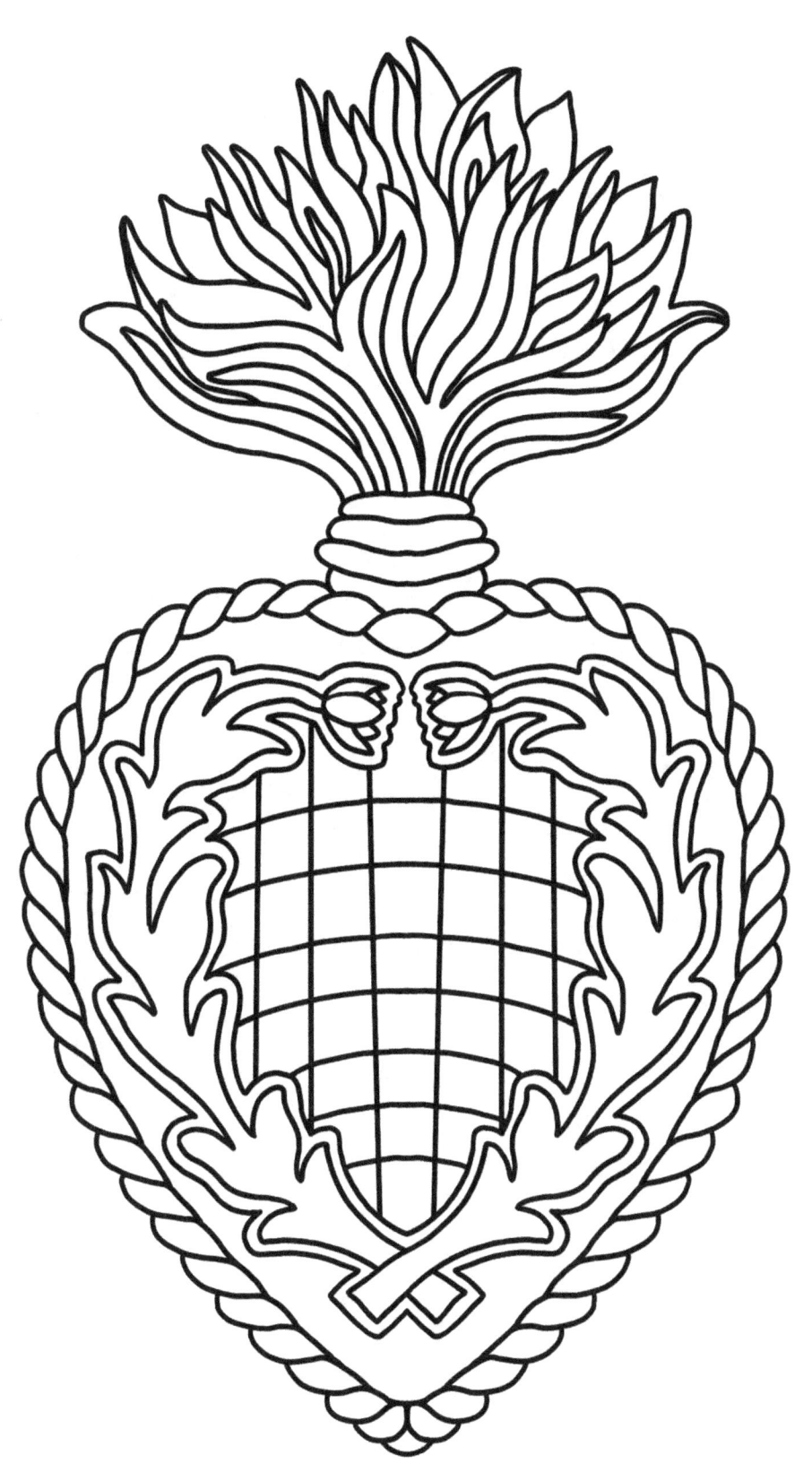

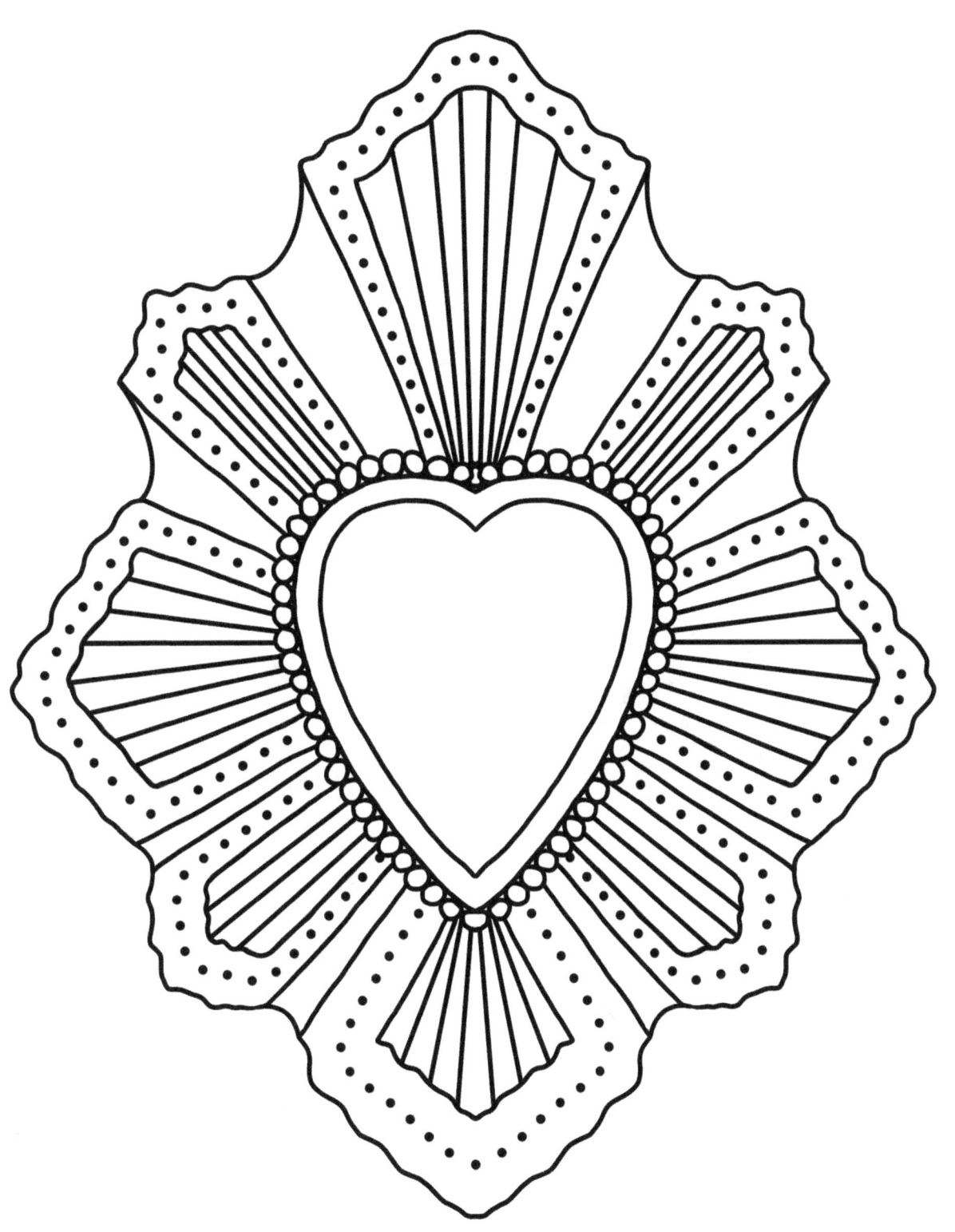

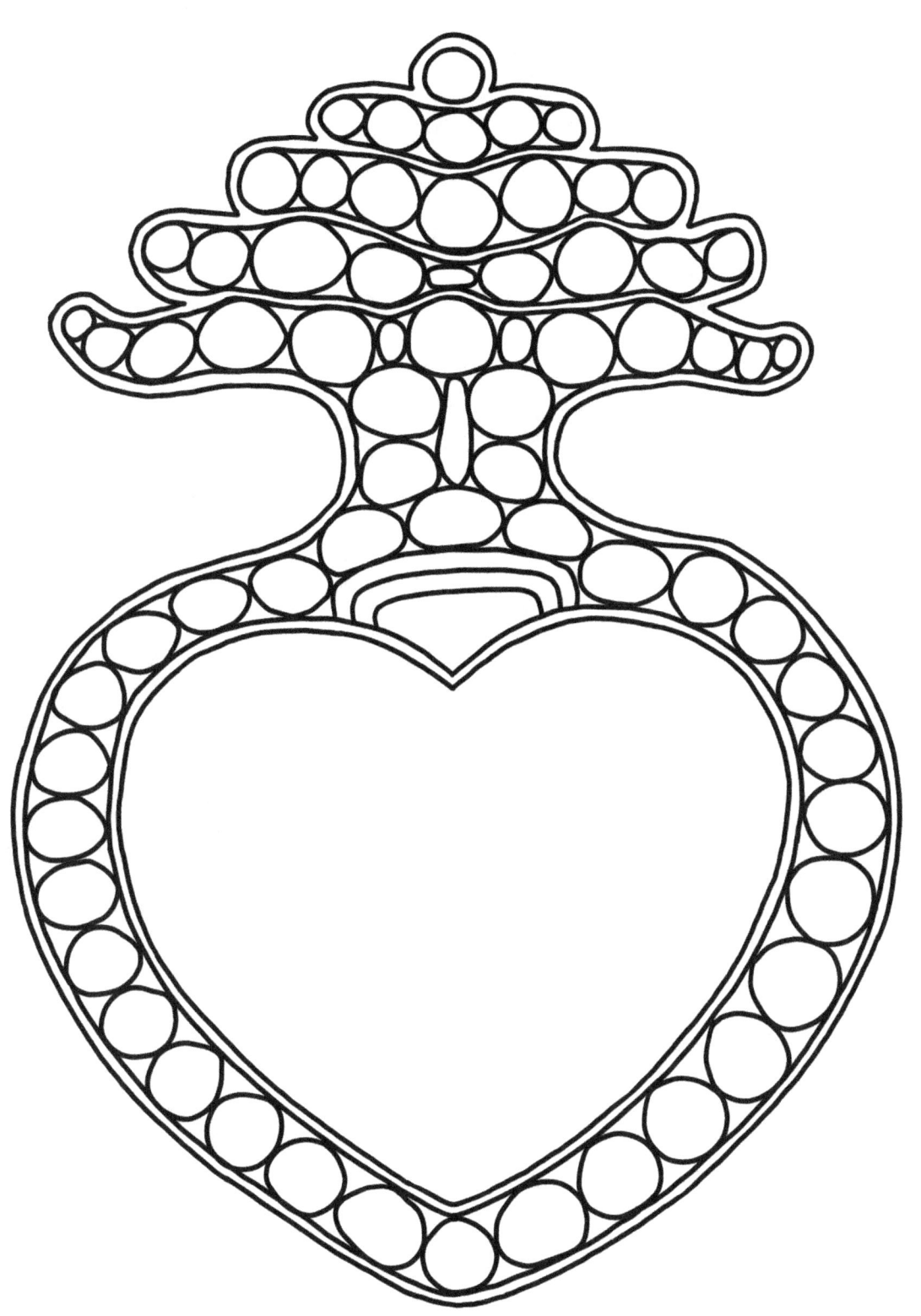

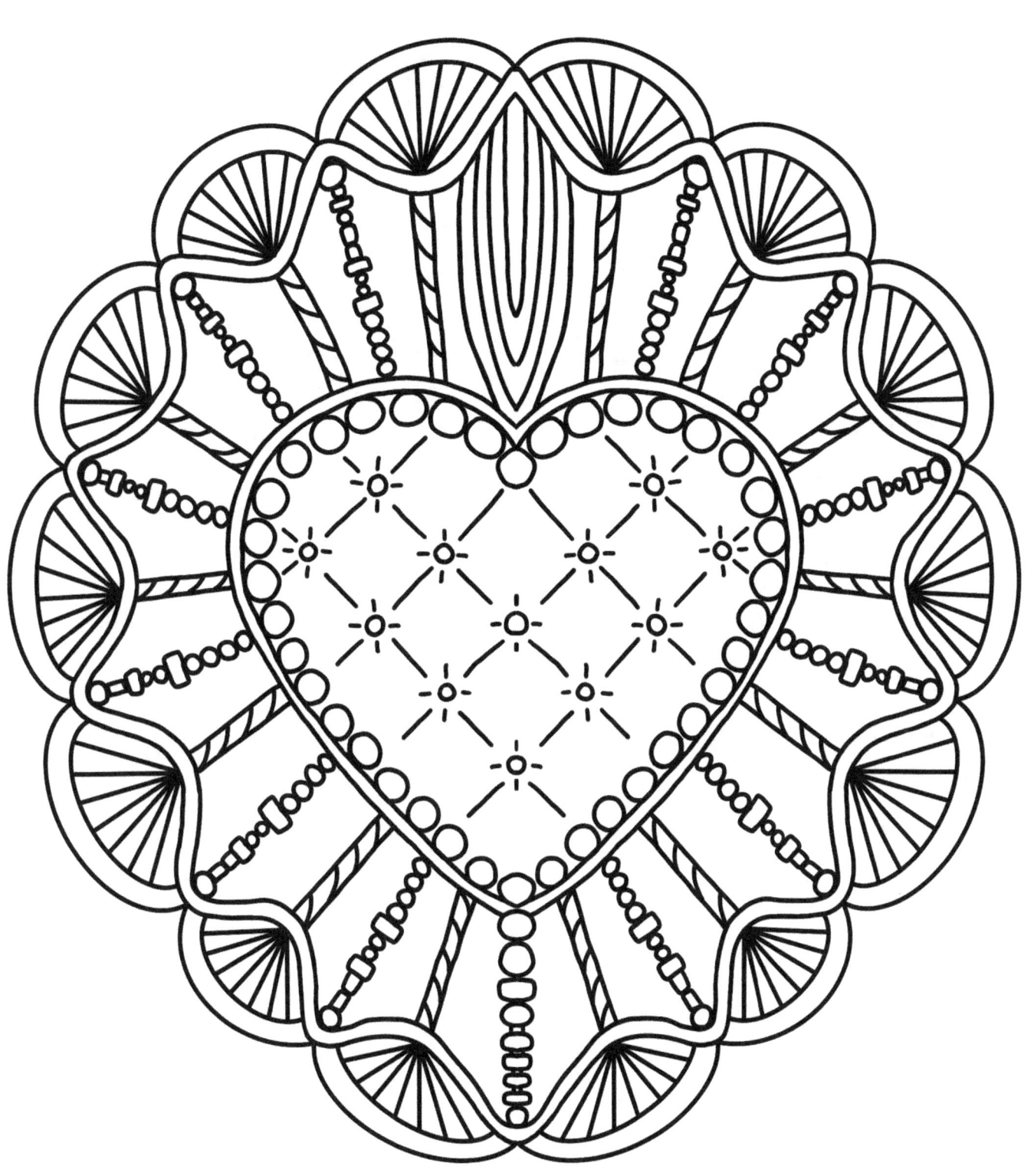

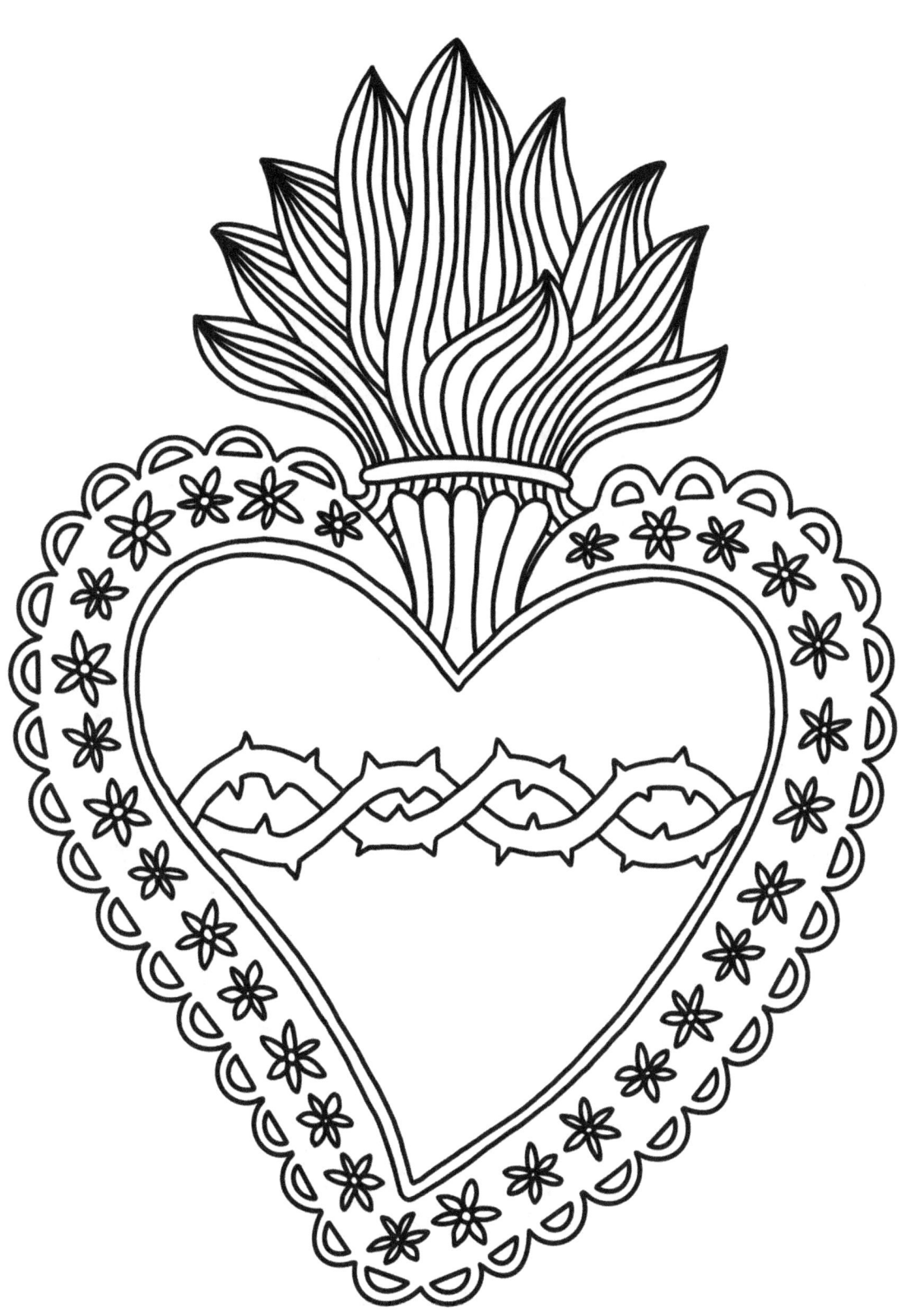

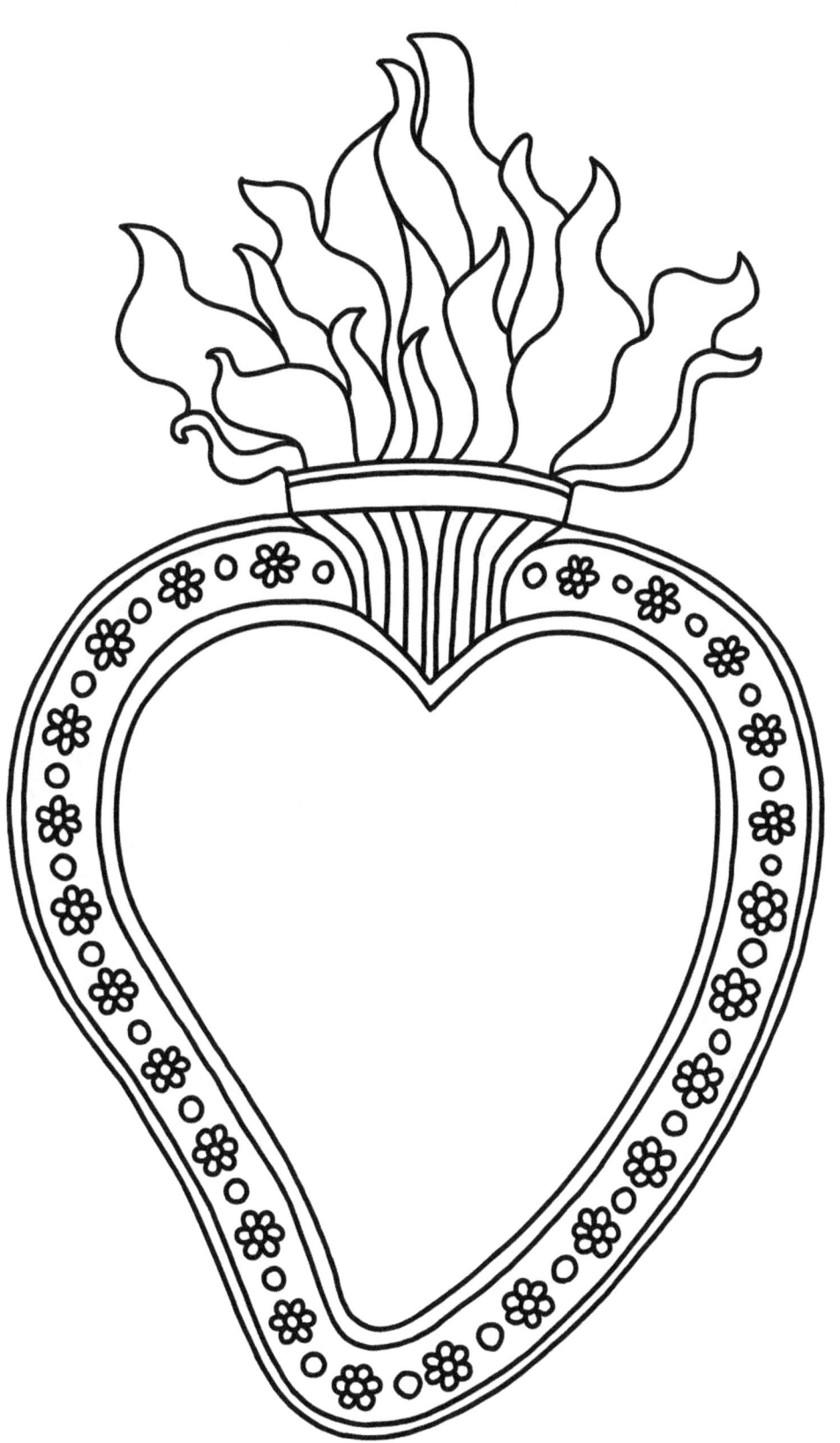

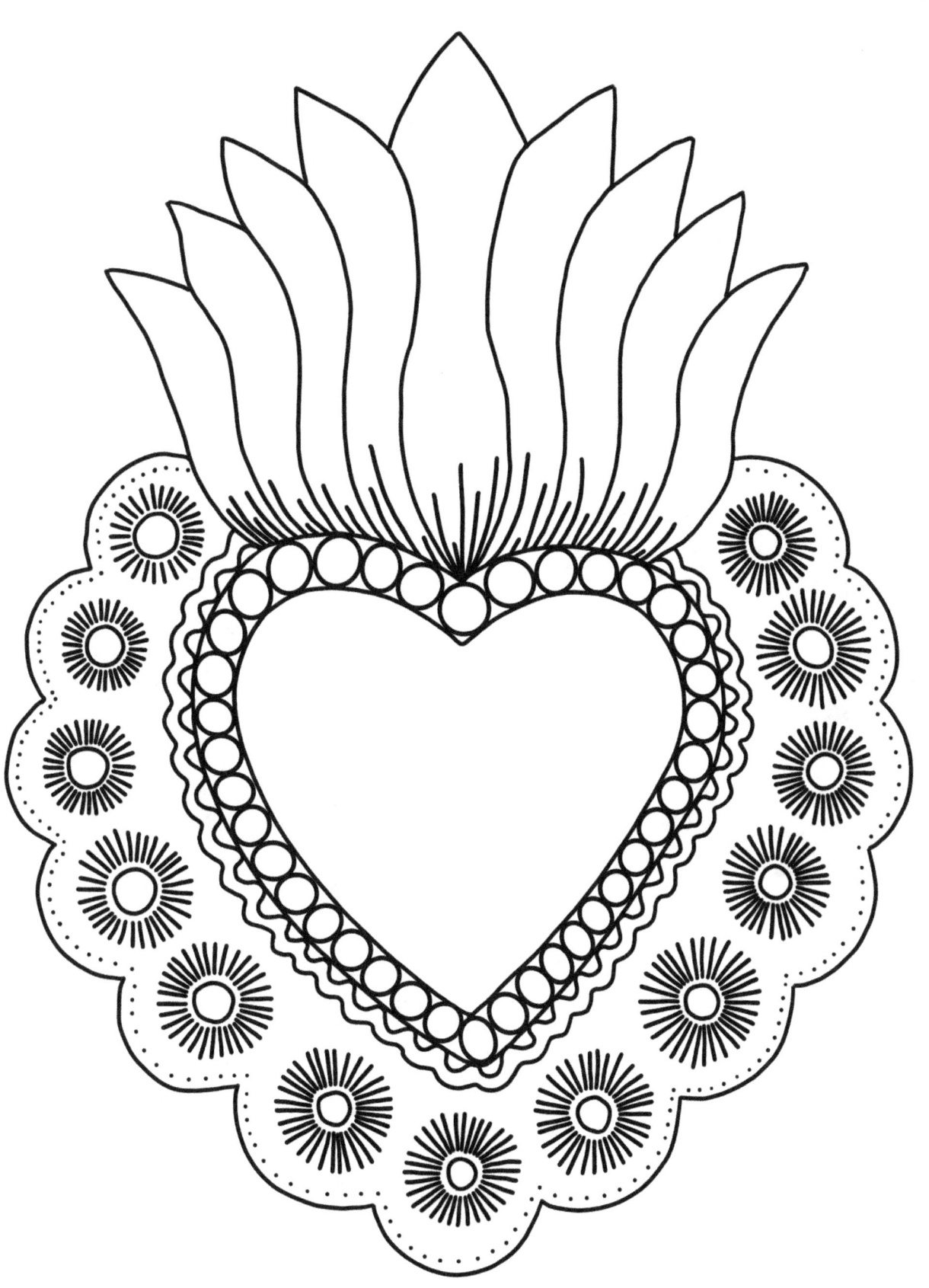

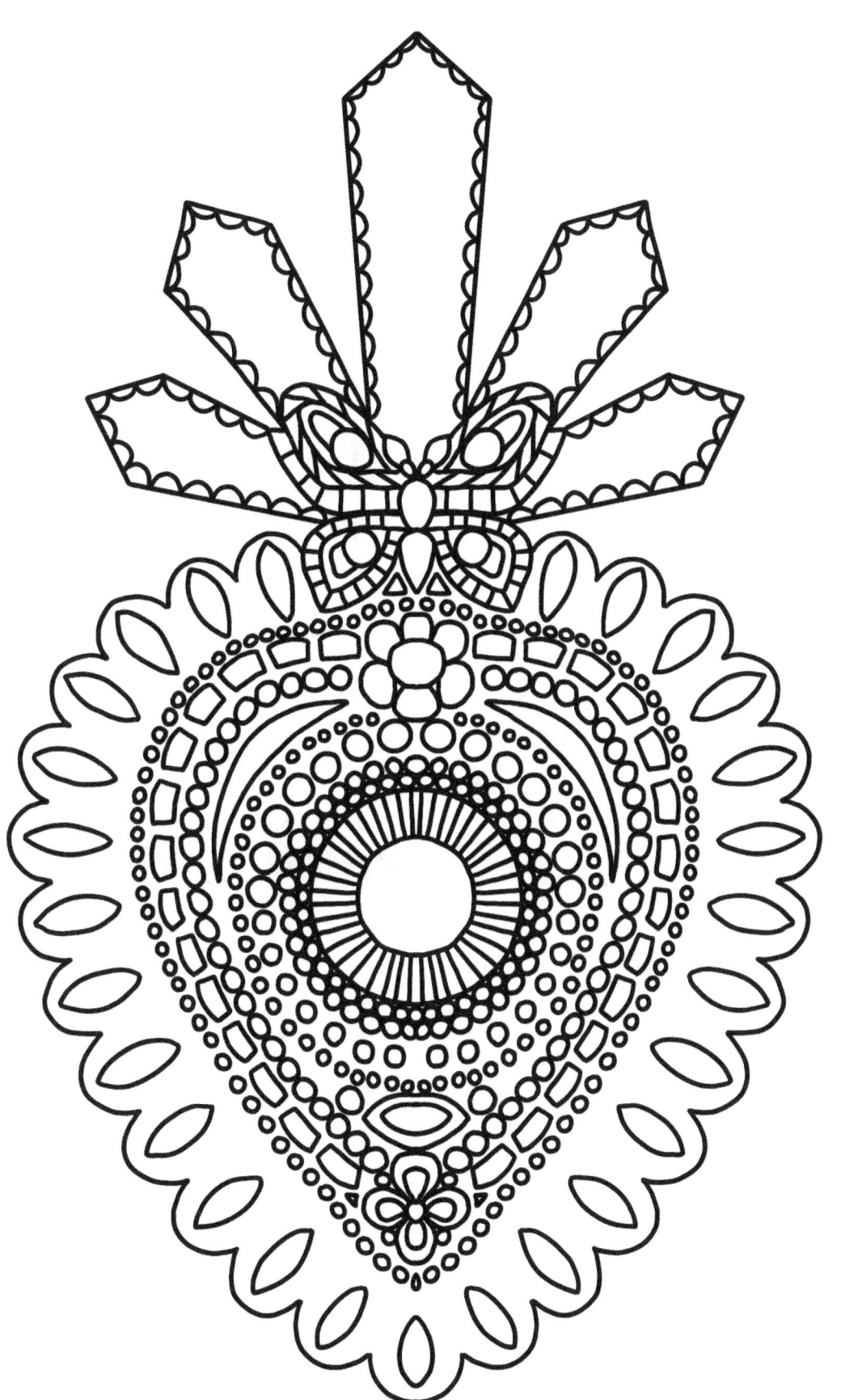

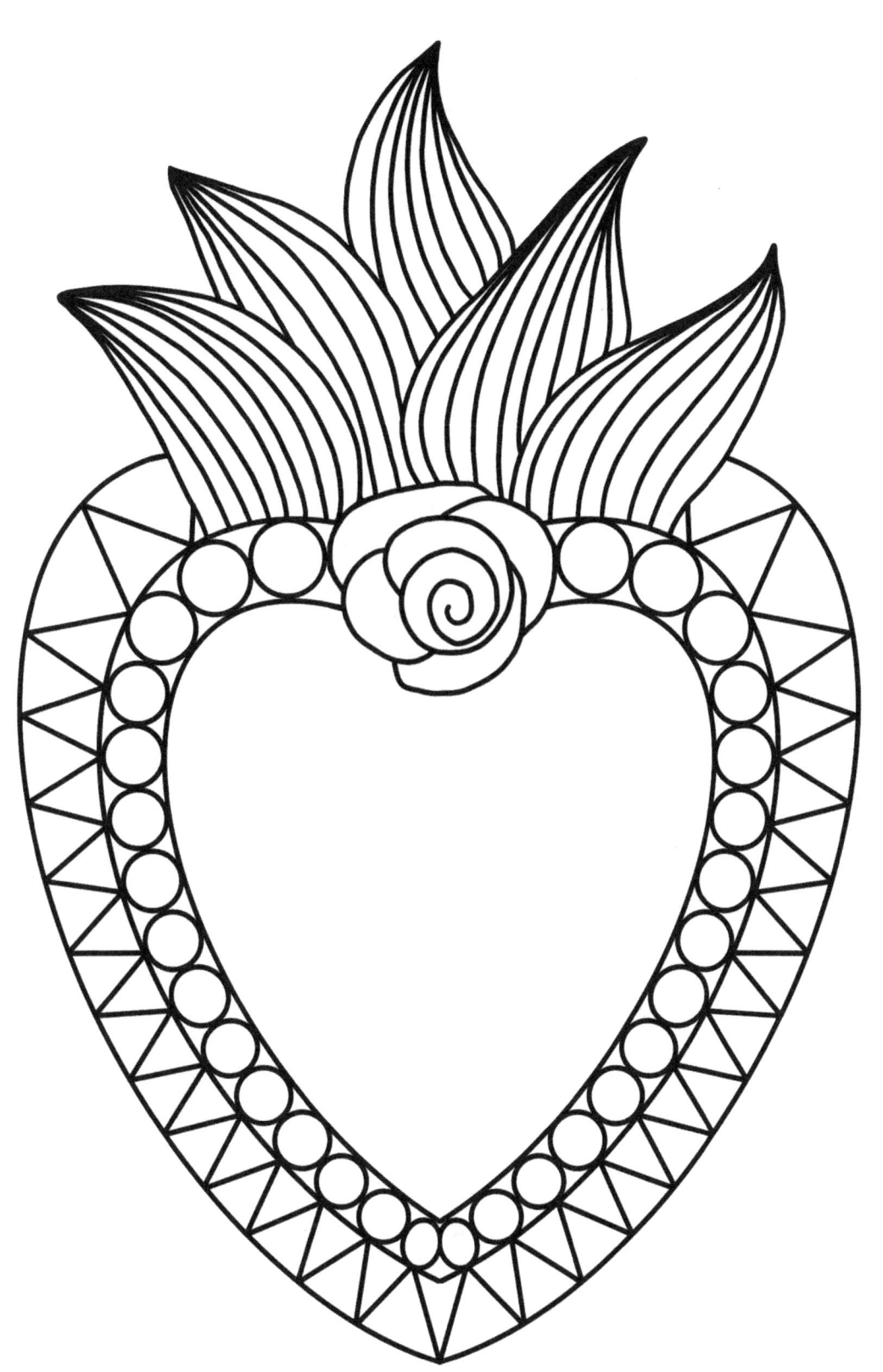

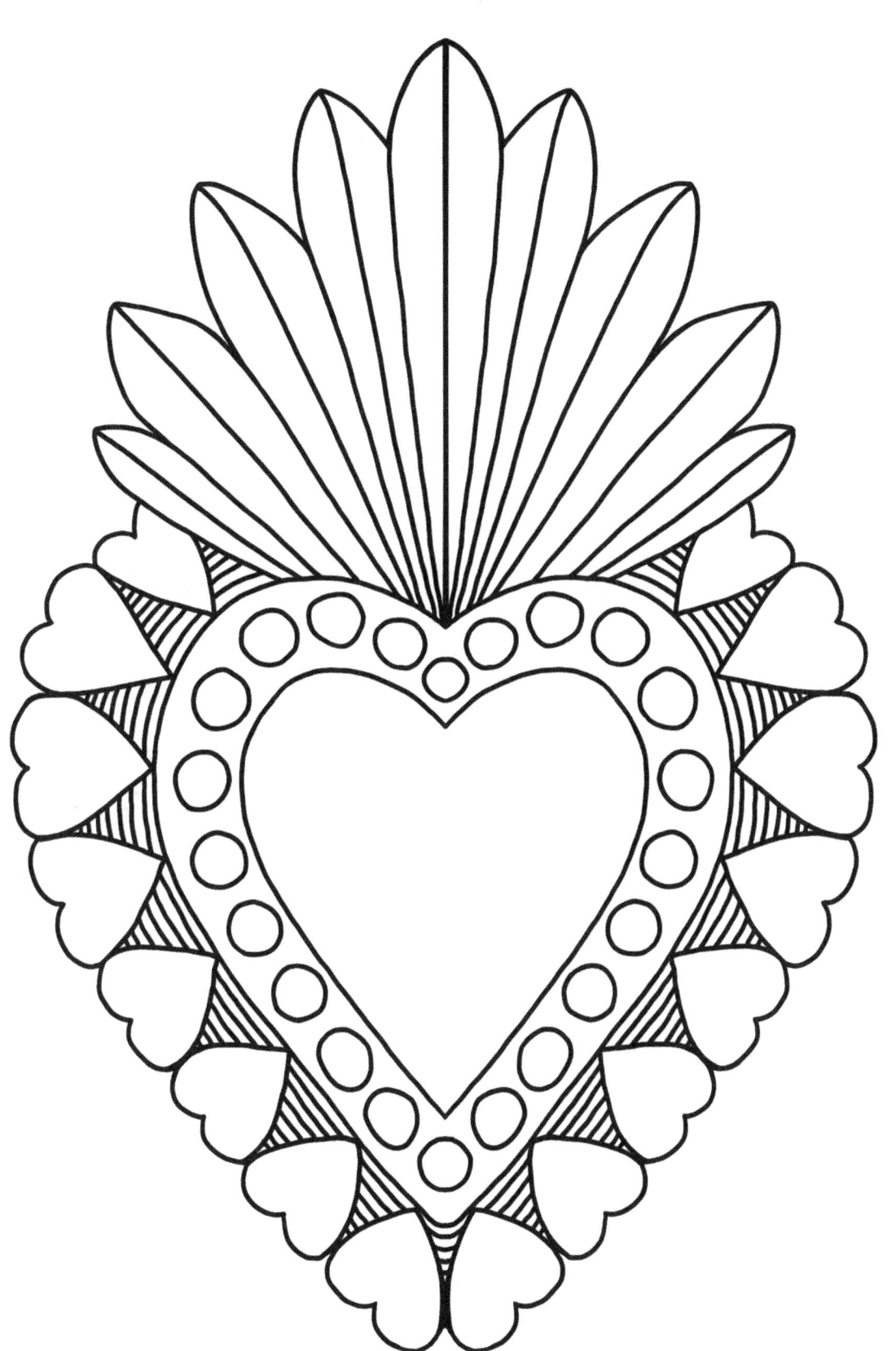

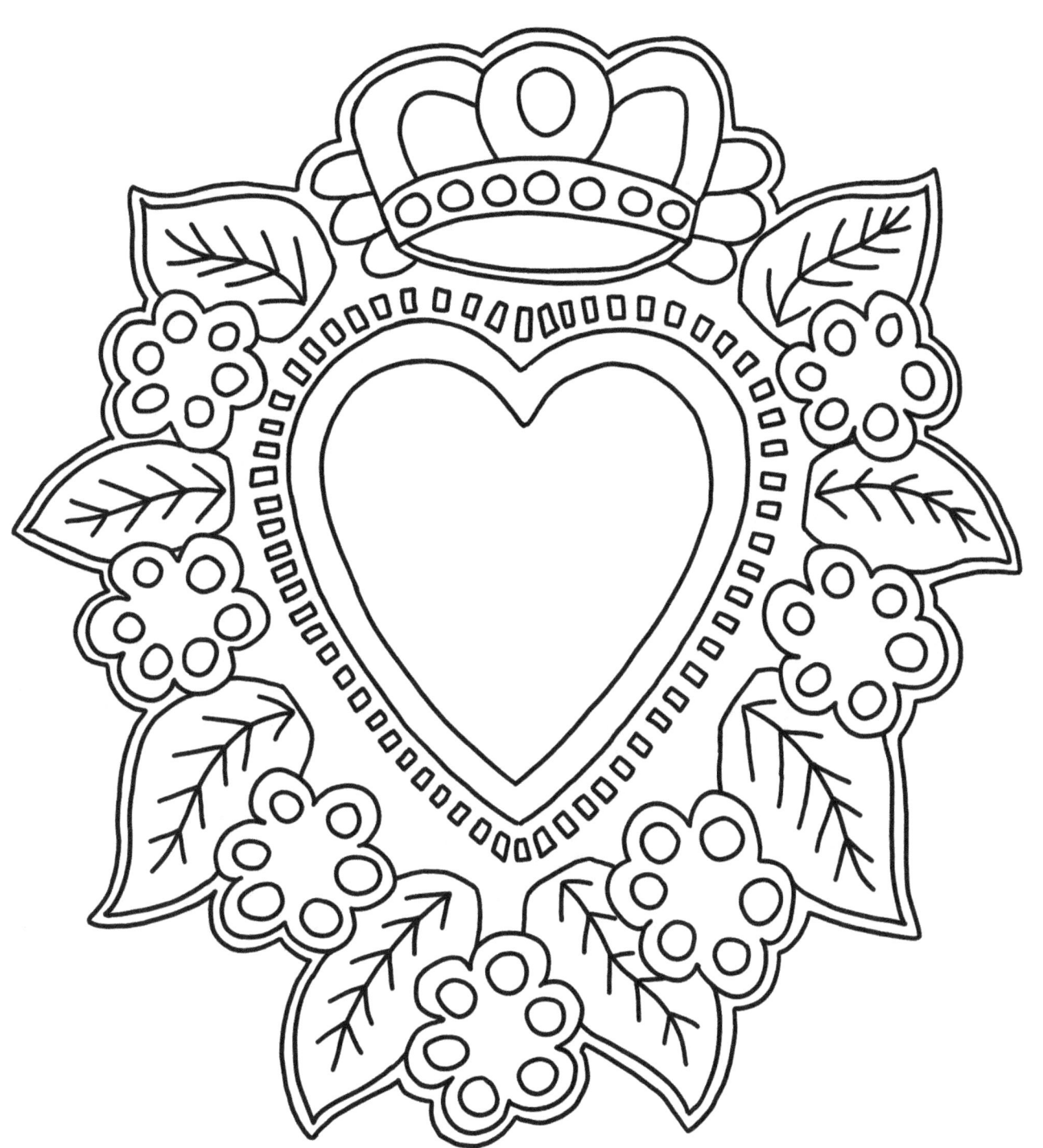

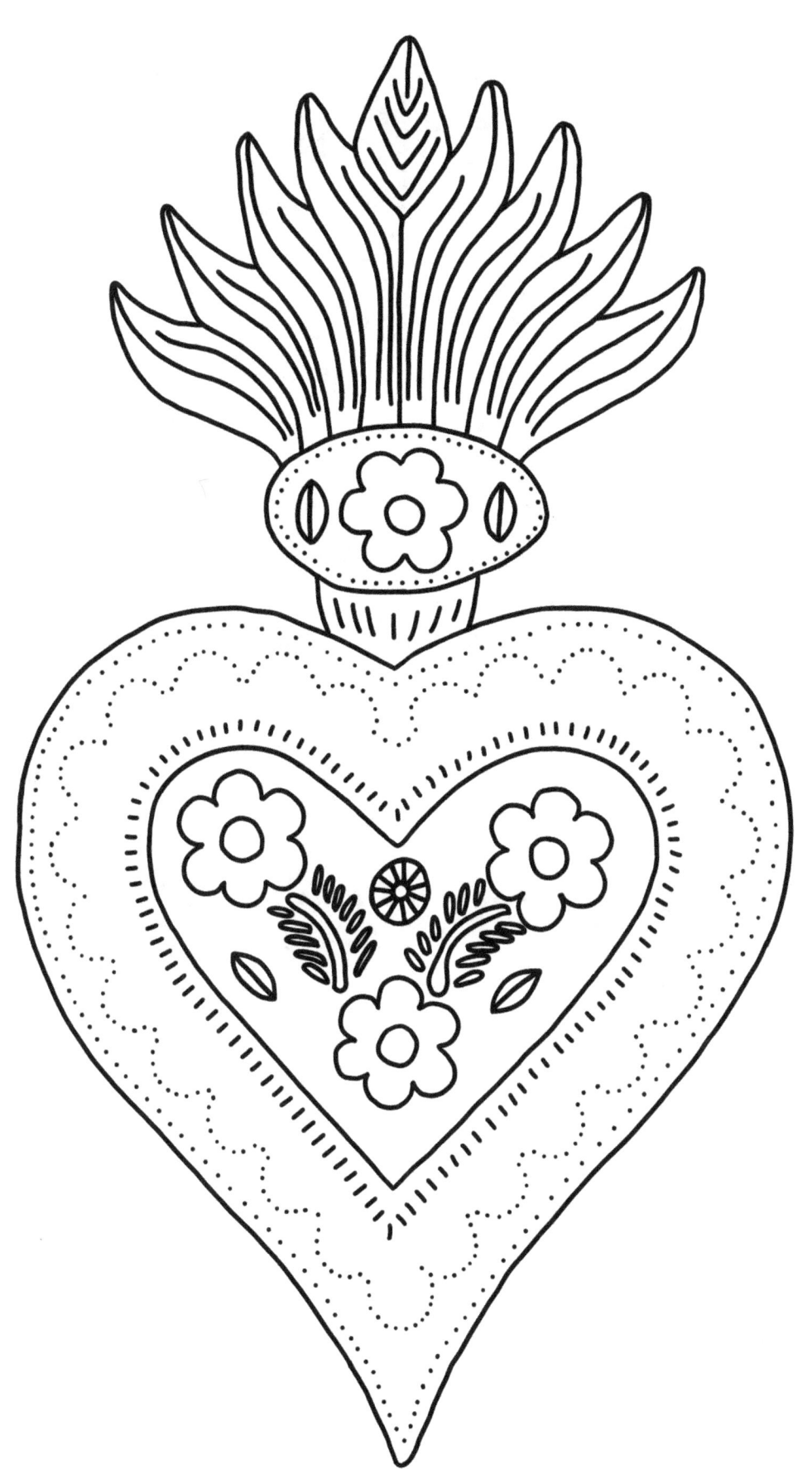

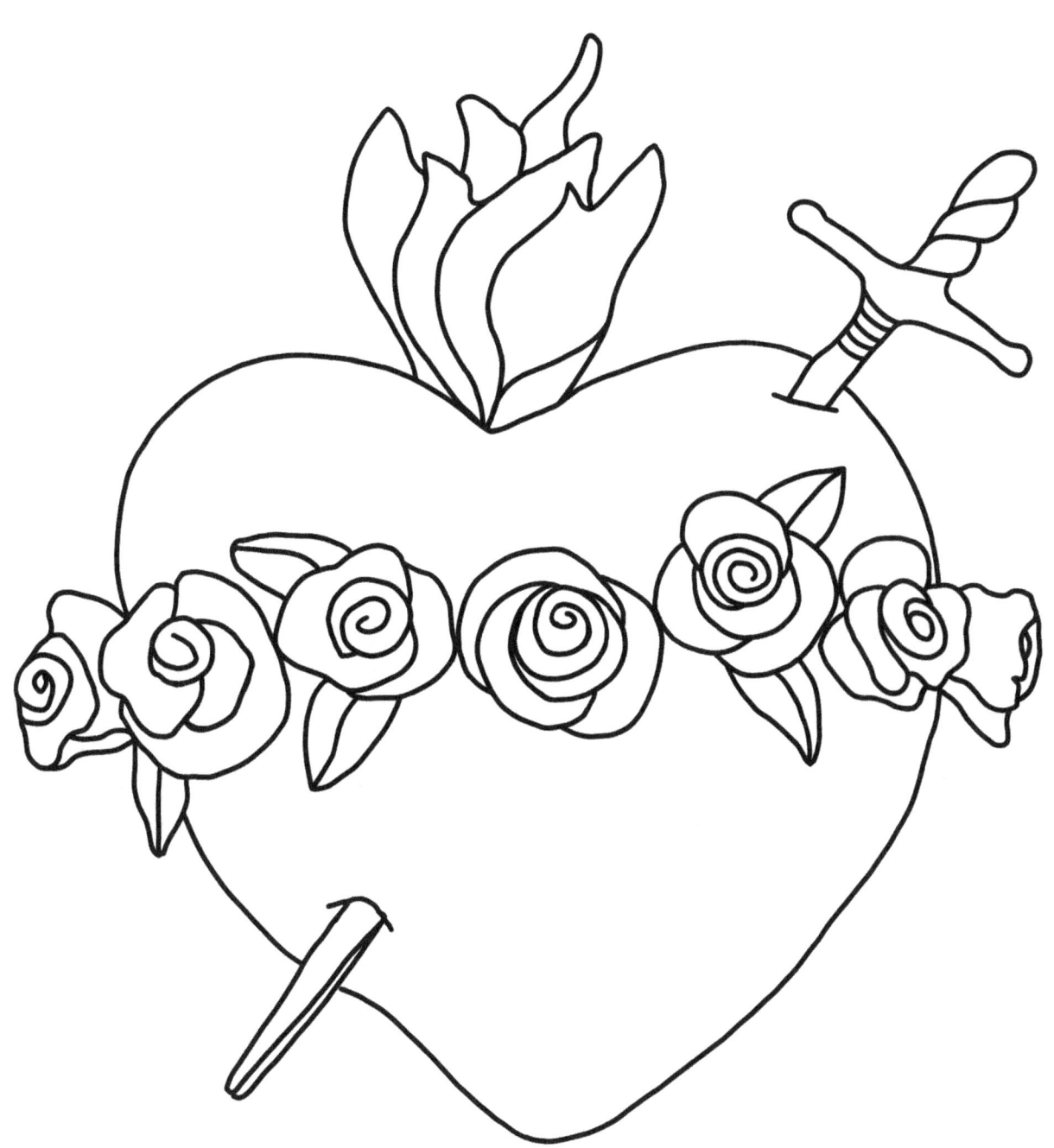

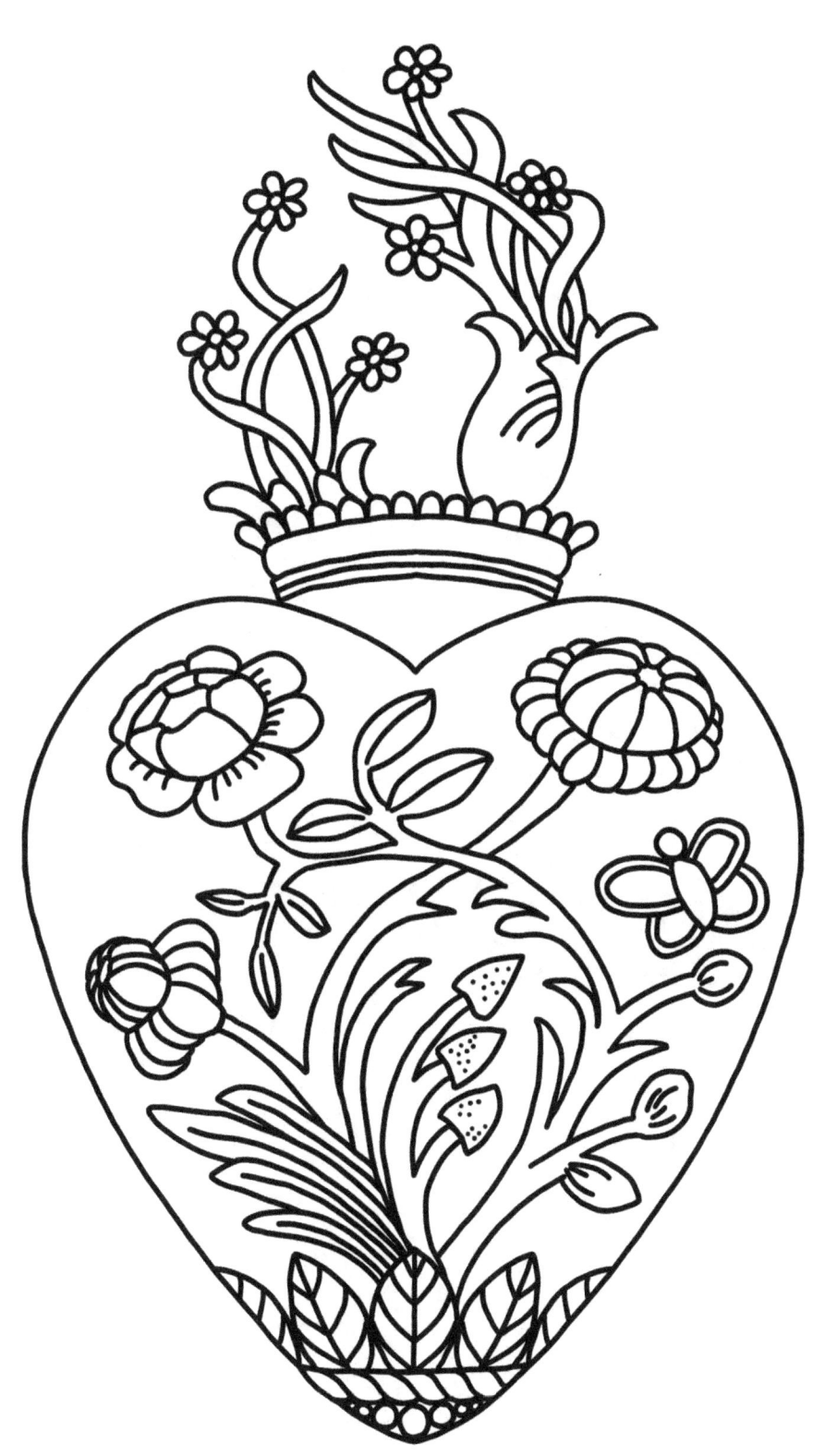

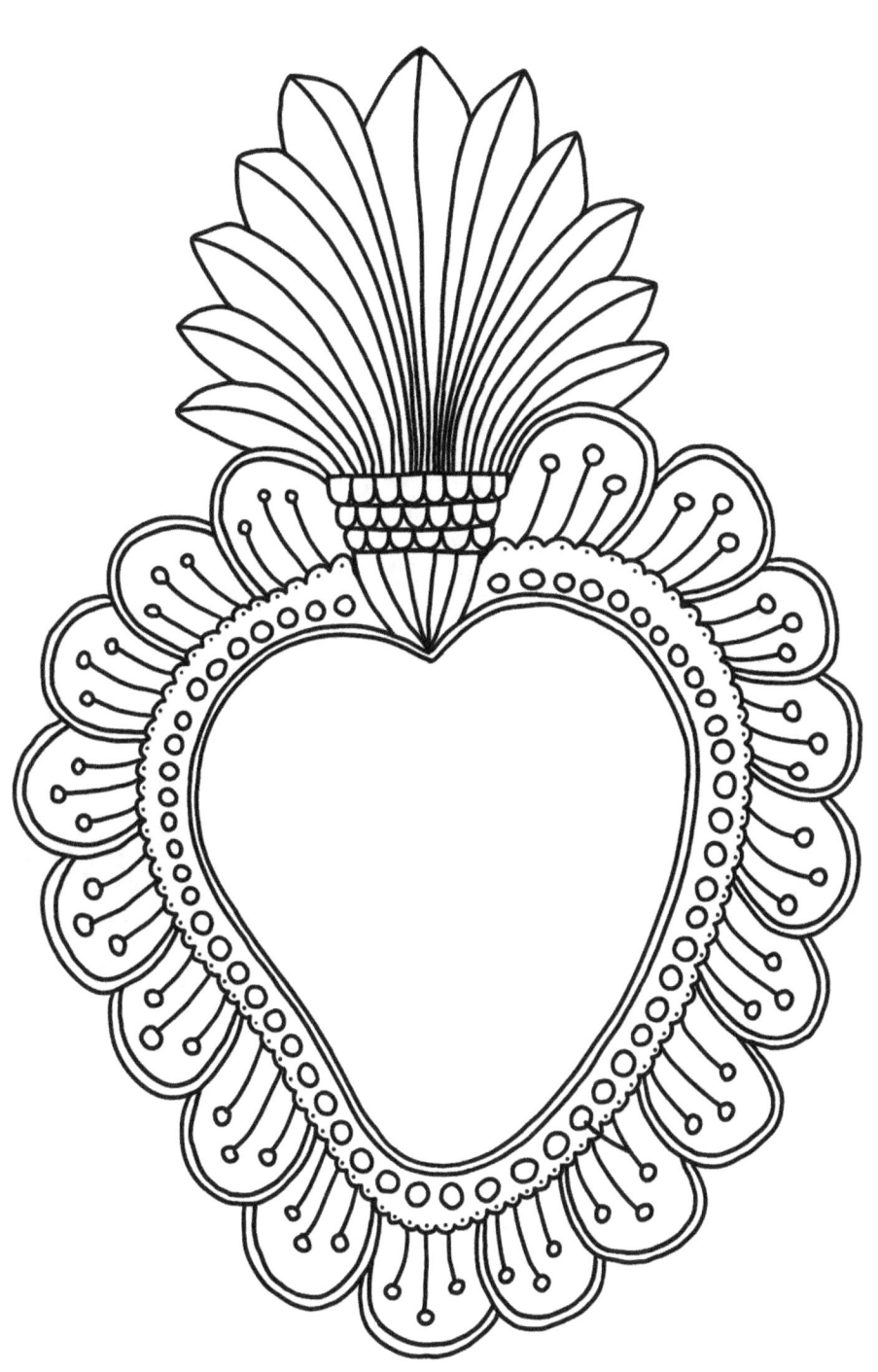

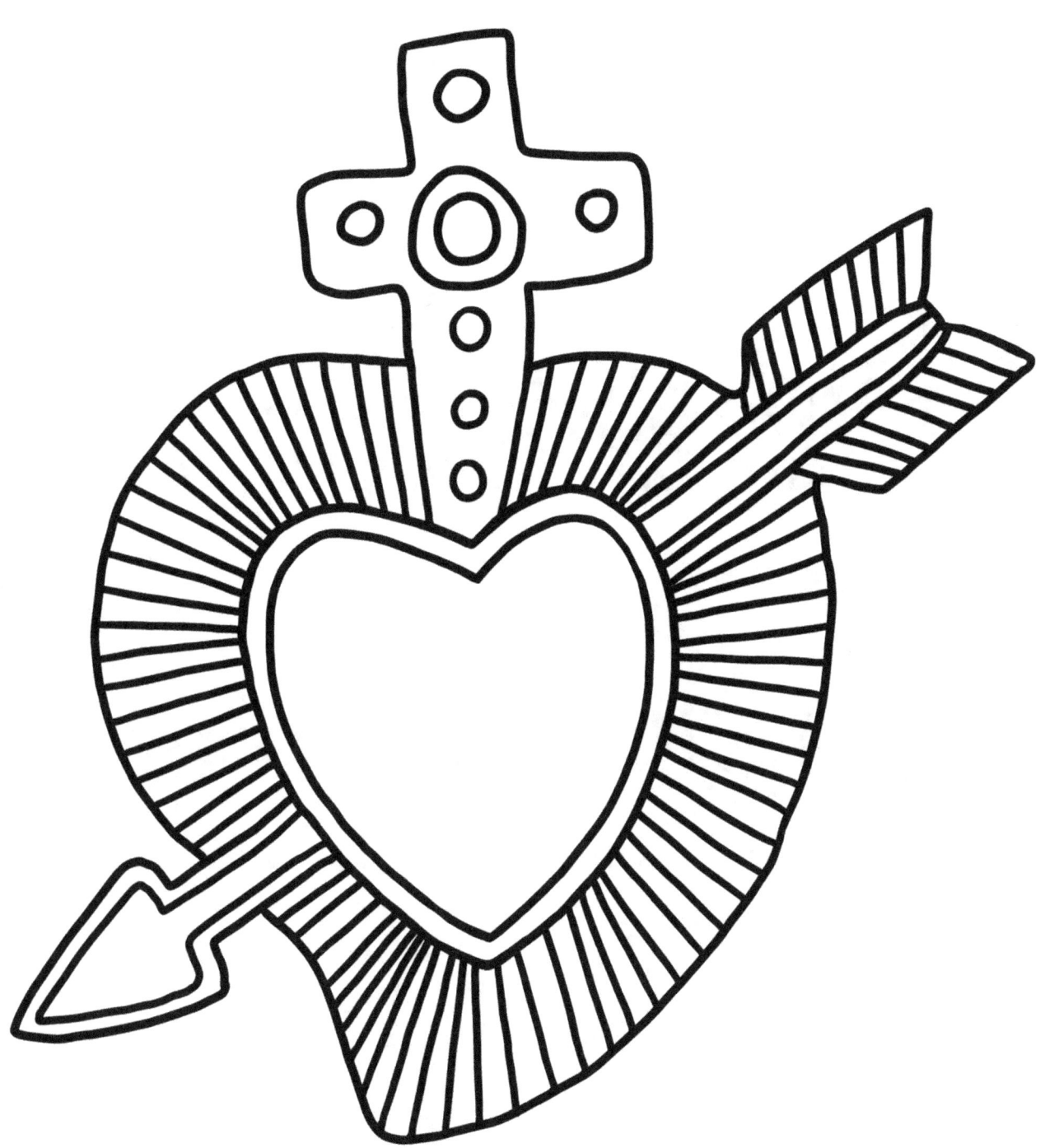

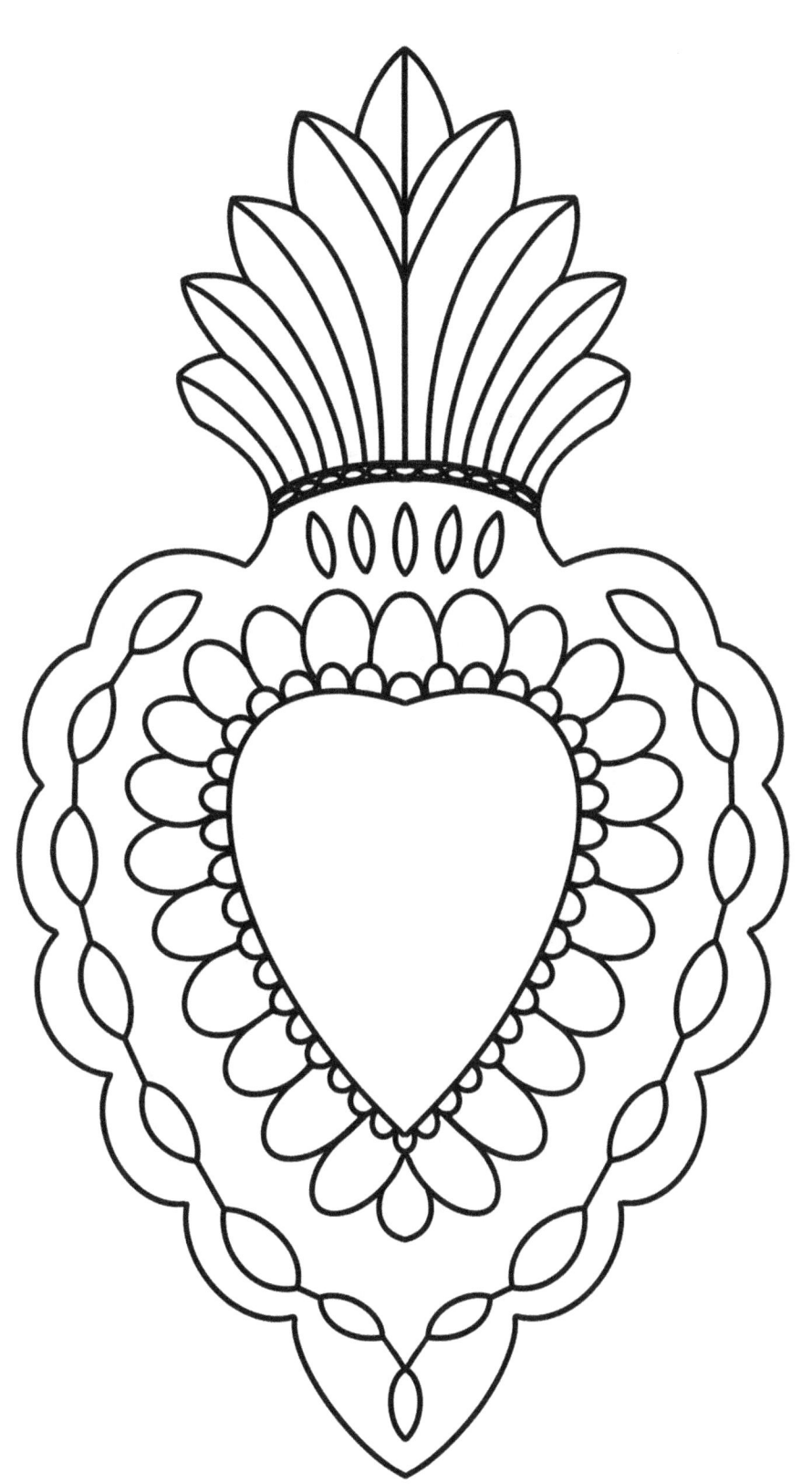

www.ingramcontent.com/pod-product-compliance
Lightning Source LLC
Chambersburg PA
CBHW080551220526
45466CB00010B/3115